THEN SOMETHING *Wondrous* HAPPENED

Unlikely encounters and unexpected graces
in search of a friendship with God

John Shaughnessy

Paxson Street Press

Published by: Paxson Street Press
Indianapolis, IN

ISBN: 978-0-578-46766-5

Cover and interior design by Jane Lee
Cover Photo by Will Barnhart, Will Barnhart Photography

Printed and bound in the United States of America

❧

*To everyone who has blessed me
with the gift of their friendship*

❧

*"The feeling remains that God
is on the journey, too."*

—St. Teresa of Avila

TABLE OF CONTENTS

INTRODUCTION

Two friends stand together at the edge of a dance floor. One looks across the room at a stranger, drawn to that person as if there is no one else in the world. The other friend notices the mesmerized stare.

In a second scene, two friends stand at the edge of a small cliff, their eyes fixated on the water beneath them. One friend leans forward, anticipating the thrill of making the jump together. The other friend inches back.

In both situations, one friend turns to the other and says, "You can do this. Trust me. I'm here for you."

These three affirmations define the essence of a close friend—someone who is there for us in our times of doubt, uncertainty and fear, someone who also invites us to embrace the breathtaking possibilities of life and love. Even more so, these three affirmations define the essence of the unique and deep friendship that God offers all of us, assuring us of his support, his love and his faith in us at every point of our lives.

In many ways, God makes his goodness and grace known in the world through our friendships. Our closest friends welcome us, lift us and accept us as who we are, with all our faults and limitations. They stand by us when we reach the edges of life, love and faith. Our best friends also encourage, inspire and challenge us to reach for something more in our lives.

God takes this gift of friendship to an even higher level. He offers his friendship to each of us, and he offers it unconditionally. No matter what, God accepts us with all his mercy and love. He's always there for us, even in our darkest times. He invites and challenges us to deepen the purpose of our lives, our bonds with other people, and our relationship with him.

The gift of friendship—the human and the divine—is at the heart of *Then Something Wondrous Happened*. The stories in this collection feature friendships that begin with surprising encounters between strangers; friendships that add joy, hope, humor and healing to life; friendships that reveal the humanity that connects us through even the toughest of times *and* the grace that God provides when we need it the most—in ways we never expect. The stories also capture the stunning gift that God extends to us, a friendship marked by his desire to walk through this life with us while inviting us to share an eternal life with him.

Then Something Wondrous Happened celebrates the life-changing quality of all these friendships. The stories of these special relationships also offer an invitation and a challenge to each of us: Move to the edge, step forward and take the leap into a friendship with God.

It's a friendship forever marked by the faith God has in us, and the love he gives us.

"You can do this. Trust me. I'm here for you."

THEN
SOMETHING
Wondrous
HAPPENED

LIGHT THE DARKNESS

The urgency in the young man's voice—plus the two questions he asked—immediately grabbed my attention.

At the time, I was part of a group of family and friends with Notre Dame loyalties, standing near the players' tunnel outside Notre Dame Stadium. It was the early evening of August 30—a short while after the Irish won their 2014 football season opener against Rice University. Involved in another conversation, I heard the young man's voice before I saw him. In a tone that was both polite and urgent, he asked someone in our group about the location of the Grotto, the shrine on Notre Dame's campus that honors the Blessed Mother.

Turning toward him, I saw that he was a blond-haired, athletic guy in a warm-up suit with a distinctive, scripted "R"—for Rice—on his jacket. But most of all, I noticed the combination of concern and desire that marked his face as he asked, "Do you think I can get there and back in 20 minutes?"—the time he said he had before the Rice team buses would be ready to leave from the stadium.

Watching and listening to him, it struck me that he didn't just *want* to get to the Grotto, he *needed* to get there. As someone who believes my life has been blessed in many ways by the intercession of Mary, I felt touched by that need. And so in a split-second reaction that I can only credit to the Holy Spirit, I told the young man, "Let's go. I'll take you there." Then we both began running—something I had only started to do a few months earlier after too many years of too little exercise. I just hoped I could keep up with him.

As we ran, he told me his name was James Hairston. When I asked him if he had played in the game that afternoon, he said he was the kicker for Rice. I mentioned that I noticed that he had made the sign of the cross every time he kicked during the game. He said he's "a devout Catholic," and he went on to tell me he had graduated from a Catholic high school in Dallas. Then he shared the two reasons he desperately wanted to visit the Grotto—reasons that nearly stopped me in my tracks.

He told me, "I have a special devotion to the Blessed Mother." As we kept stride, he shared with me that his mother had died of skin cancer when he was 13, and how her death had devastated him.

James also said that shortly after his mother's death, the Blessed Mother appeared to him in a vision and told him that she would be his mother from that moment.

He then talked about how much it would mean to him to light a candle at the Grotto for his mother and the Blessed Mother.

As we continued running, he noticed a side view of the Blessed Mother atop Notre Dame's Golden Dome and exclaimed, "That's so beautiful!" He asked if I had graduated from Notre Dame. I told him long ago, and that one of our sons was a graduate, too, and our daughter was a senior there this year.

James said, "I would have loved to come here."

Soon, we were at the side steps leading down to the Grotto, a setting that has long been a touchstone in my life. And when we stood in front of the shrine, James' face lit up.

Before going inside the railing to light a candle, James handed me his smart phone and asked me to take some pictures to preserve this moment. Knowing my inexperience with camera phones, I approached someone younger standing nearby, told him the details of James' story about his mother and the Blessed Mother, and asked him to use James' phone to take pictures—which he did.

As James lit a candle for his mother and the Blessed Mother, he was so focused on what he was doing that he never looked in the direction of the camera. He then moved to the prayer railing in front of the shrine, pulled a small statue of the Blessed Mother from his backpack, placed it on the railing, and began to pray. Every move he made was touched with an earnest love and reverence.

When James finished his prayers and rose from the kneeling pad, his face beamed with a glow of peace and joy. Before we left the Grotto, James looked around one more time. It was clear the difference his several minutes there had made.

During our return to the stadium, he continued to tell me about his life. He talked about how life is sometimes a struggle. He mentioned how he helped lead a teammate to God.

James also talked about a conversation he had with a priest from his high school days, a priest in his 40s who had been diagnosed with terminal cancer. He shared how the priest told him how grateful to God he is for all the joy he has been given in life. James also noted that he wears a brown scapular the priest gave him.

Sharing one more story, James described the horrible car accident that his younger brother was in earlier in 2014—and how his brother came out of the wreck without a cut or injury.

I told James, "I think your mother and the Blessed Mother took care of him." James agreed.

As we neared the stadium, James stopped to give me his e-mail address and to type mine into his phone so we could keep in touch. Moments later, we were back near the players' tunnel. I prepared to give James a quick goodbye, knowing he needed to re-join his teammates and coaches. Instead, he asked, "Do you have time to pray?" I said, "Sure." As he began a Hail Mary, our voices soon blended. When we finished the prayer, James continued, thanking God and the Blessed Mother for the time we shared, for the blessings of life.

Standing there together, I thought about how just 20 minutes earlier James and I were strangers. Now, we were connected forever by the grace of Mary. When it came time to say goodbye, we hugged.

As I headed to meet with family and friends, I kept thinking of James, his mother and the Blessed Mother. I kept thinking of how his two mothers must be filled with joy, pride and love for their son.

Less than an hour later, James sent me an e-mail. It read, "I will never forget that moment."

Neither will I.

⊹

Invitation/Challenge: I like to think of the Blessed Mother as "The Queen of Unlikely Encounters and Unexpected Graces." Start with the defining moment of Mary's life. An angel appears to Mary and tells her that she, who has never had relations with anyone, will become the mother of God's son. We tend to take that story for granted now, but let it sink in. An angel appears to Mary and tells her that she will become the mother of God's son. It is the most unlikely encounter imaginable, and yet it leads to so many unexpected graces for her—and for everyone whose life is touched by her and her son.

God and the Blessed Mother have continued that approach of unlikely encounters and unexpected graces ever since. Sometimes, it happens in moments that gain worldwide notice, such as when she appeared to three shepherd children in a field in Fatima. Other times, it happens in small moments, such as when two strangers meet outside a football stadium. In all such moments, Mary is making it known that she is a continuing presence in our lives. She is also calling us to look beyond ourselves—to God, to other people.

Every day, God and the Blessed Mother place people in our lives. These encounters will usually arise in familiar situations—home, work or school—with family and friends. Then there are the opportunities that come unexpectedly—a call from a long-lost friend or a request for help from a stranger. Each of these encounters puts us in the presence of people who have hopes and dreams, burdens and vulnerabilities. Each of these encounters presents us with an opportunity to give light to their life. Just as often, these encounters have a way of changing our life. Our darkness is illuminated by the light of the other person.

The best part of my experience with James Hairston is that we still keep in touch. We have become friends. In one of the notes that James occasionally sends me, he wrote: "My Dad used to tell us kids that there are people in life that God uses to reveal himself. Those kinds of people expect nothing in return. They answer a call and deliver a message. My Dad told me and my three siblings that those people are angels."

In keeping with James' note about angels, let us remember this: More than 2,000 years ago, an angel appeared to Mary and she said yes, giving birth to a son. Now, we live in a time when Mary and her son ask us to be their angels. They ask us to offer hope and healing to others, to light their darkness, to share our friendship. We get that opportunity often in our lives, sometimes through unlikely encounters with strangers. When we do, let us dare to say yes. And when you do say yes, just be ready—for the unexpected graces that will follow.

Who is that someone—a family member, a friend, a stranger in need—who God and the Blessed Mother have placed in your life, hoping you will make a difference?

Light the darkness.

LAUGH WITH GOD

Jane Crady calls God "strange"—in an affectionate way.
She also says, "I just laugh with God now. I say, 'You have
such a sense of humor.'"

It's not the reaction that some people might expect from
a grandmother who has dedicated her life to helping people
whose lives have been devastated by some of the worst
hurricanes in American history, by floods, and by tornadoes
that damaged hundreds of homes and left people dead. Yet
while Crady has seen disaster and devastation in horrific ways,
she has also witnessed hope and help in generous supply as
a coordinator of disaster preparedness and response for a
Catholic Charities agency.

She also believes she has experienced the touch of God.

"I see miracles every day," she says. "When you go in with a
servant's heart and just want to help, miracles do happen. And
God sends people. He's so strange. He really is. One time, there
was a gal, and we were pretty much done with fixing her house
after Hurricane Katrina. But the tile needed to be laid on the
floors. And we couldn't find anybody that had tile experience.
And so she and I were sitting under a tree talking about this,
and my phone rang. I said, 'Excuse me, honey.'

"It was a call from a guy who's volunteering. He's coming
from Missouri. And he's by himself. He asks if I could put him
to work. I said, "What kind of work do you do?' He said, 'I'm a
tile man.' It happens all the time like that. It really does. I just
laugh with God now. I say, 'You have such a sense of humor.'"

While Crady laughs with God, she also strives to serve as "his
hands and his feet" to others. When two young parents and their
four children lost their poorly-constructed home in a flood,
they began living in a small, run-down RV that they borrowed.
Learning about their situation, Crady helped the father, a manual

laborer, find a job. Then she led the effort to rebuild the house, including the construction of an addition to it.

"The biggest thing we can give anybody is hope. But we have to be very careful," she says. "There are people who come in right away to help and promise things, and then they are gone. People give false hope, and that's very, very hurtful. So when you can offer hope and know that you can deliver it, it makes the difference. You never promise anything. You always say, 'I can't promise you anything, darling, but I will do everything in my power to give you the help you need.'

"The spiritual part is huge, too. A lot of people do blame God: 'Why did he do this to me?' When you can sit and be with them and guide them through, it helps. And when you're about halfway through the rebuilding, you start to watch the transformation of these people. You start to see them smile again, shine again and go back to church again.

"It's so rewarding. You just form these wonderful relationships with people you've helped. It's heartbreaking for sure, but you know as long as the hope is there, the rewards and the little miracles are going to happen. That's what keeps you going."

So does the joy of laughing with God. She recalls a time when she prayed for a bulldozer that she desperately needed to help others.

"The next thing you know someone is driving up with a bulldozer," she says with a smile. The smile turns to a laugh and her eyes light up, thinking about God.

✝

Invitation/Challenge: I have a friend who tells jokes to God. It's a tradition he carries on from his father, who believed that God hears so many pleas for help and stories of sadness in a day that he could use an extra laugh or a smile. In that moment when he shares his joke, my friend says he feels closer to God and his father.

I also know someone who reaches for two cups when he prepares to spend time with God. He fills one of the cups for himself and the other for God. Then he takes them to a table where he invites God to sit across from him—two friends sharing time and a drink. His two-cup tradition gives him a concrete focus on God during their time together. He says that God, just through listening, always re-fills his cup by the end of their shared time.

Other friends prefer a more traditional approach. They spend time with God in a chapel or a church, listening for his voice in their silence.

Each of us has our own way of inviting God into our lives. Each of us can find our own way to a friendship with God. Of course, for many of us, the thought of having a friendship with God and laughing with God is a hard concept to embrace. Some of us view our relationship with God in terms of a distant, almighty master and a lowly, unworthy servant. Others see God as a genie to be called upon when we want a wish or a need to be fulfilled.

Yet the precedent of a friendship with God is present in the bonds that connected Jesus and the first group of people he chose as his own, the Apostles. They traveled together, ate together and shared adventures together on a journey that lasted years. They talked about everything, from the basic concerns of what they would eat next to the deepest questions of their place in the world, their ties with each other and their connection with God. It was a full-access, 24-7, up-close-and-personal relationship marked by faith, trust and love, a relationship that Christ continued to offer even when the Apostles betrayed him, doubted him and abandoned him.

In his time with the Apostles, Christ was the essence of a best friend—someone you learn from, someone who forgives you your limitations, someone who encourages you to be the best person you can be. And in the darkest times, he finds a way to reach you, to let you know he's there for you, to give you a reason to hope—and even a reason to laugh when the world gets too overwhelming. That's how our best friends are. And God offers us that same kind of friendship—on an even higher level—just as he did to the Apostles.

Think of a moment from your life when God has been there for you as a friend, giving you just what you needed in an unexpected way that made you smile or laugh or feel comforted.

Think of a way you can invite God into your life as a friend. Laugh with God.

GIVE UP FEAR

The moment touched Father Rick Nagel as he visited Macklin Swinney in the hospital and listened to the young man share the remarkable resolution of what he was giving up for Lent.

At the time, the then-26-year-old Swinney had already been diagnosed with the most severe stage of skin cancer, and doctors had told him his odds of surviving were small. It was a dark, frightening period for Swinney. But he still wanted to make the most of whatever time he had left in his life, including making the most of his decision to be baptized and become a member of the Catholic Church.

Swinney had made that decision after joining his grandparents for Mass one Sunday at the church where Father Nagel is the pastor. Swinney had been moved that Sunday by Father Nagel's homily that focused on the themes, "God wouldn't put things in our lives if we couldn't handle them," and "everything happens for a reason even if we don't know it at the time."

Believing he was being called to God and the Church, Swinney talked to Father Nagel after the Mass. And he soon started the process to enter the Church. It was also the beginning of a powerful connection between Swinney and the priest. When his struggle with cancer forced Swinney into the hospital, Father Nagel came to visit. During one visit when they talked about Lent, Swinney shared the resolution he wanted to make.

"Out of nowhere, he said, 'I'm going to give up fear,'" Father Nagel recalled.

The priest was stunned and inspired.

"If you're faced with death as a young man, and there's not much hope of medical recovery, the natural human tendency is to be afraid. I was struck by how God had worked so beautifully in that moment to have this young man in his wisdom say, 'I'm going to give up fear.' "

Swinney would hold onto that resolution—and his life—for more than a year. During that time, he talked about what led him to first make that resolution.

"It was a scary time in my life," he said. "I was facing death. Not only that, I had a fear of what I would leave behind, what I hadn't accomplished, what I would have to go through with treatments, and how it would turn out. I decided to leave it to God. I thought if it was possible to give up fear, I would. It's been a freeing experience. Without fear, I didn't have the anxiety that loomed around all the time. It took a lot of things out of the equation. It let me focus on my life."

Swinney made the most of his time and his dreams. When his life was threatened by the return of his cancer, Father Nagel arranged for an emergency baptism for him.

"It was very powerful," Swinney said. "I had a lot of friends and family who rallied around me. It was an emotional time for me.

"I received Communion for the first time. I'll never forget my first Communion. I don't know what it was about it, but it definitely touched something inside of me."

During that year, the people closest to Swinney noticed the change that his faith had on him. Just as important, they knew the impact that his life had on them.

"Macklin has always reveled in life," said his mother, Maureen Murphy, during that time. "He just gives 100 percent to whatever he does. He's always been a joy. His strength comes from wrapping his arms around whatever matters to him. He's embracing his faith and his spirituality like every other joy he's found in his life."

Swinney's girlfriend saw the difference, too.

"I knew his belief in God and Jesus Christ was important to him, but it's become even more important in the past year," said Callie Bontrager. "I've told him, 'I can hold the hope for you, if you need me to.' There haven't been many times when he's asked me to do that."

That's because Swinney spent that year giving doses of faith, hope and inspiration to others. He kept that approach to life even after his doctor told him there was nothing more that could be done for him. A few weeks later, Swinney died on Good Friday.

During the funeral Mass, Father Nagel recalled the last time he saw Swinney. The priest visited his friend in the house of his grandparents—Don and Kathleen Murphy—where a hospice setting had been created.

"We prayed the rosary with him," Father Nagel told Swinney's family and friends who filled the church. "At the end, he said to me, 'God bless you, Father.' " Touched by that memory, Father Nagel became emotional as he added, "That's the kind of love this young man had. He was always blessing others."

Father Nagel considers it appropriate that Swinney died on Good Friday: "He knew the cross of Christ. He embraced the cross of Christ. Macklin knew the suffering of Christ on the cross."

After a pause, the priest said, "It would also be appropriate to continue to celebrate Easter. We don't just die. We rise again."

Swinney embraced that belief in life even as he faced the reality of his death. Through it all, he blazed a legacy of light in the darkest times of life.

Father Nagel touched upon that legacy as he remembered the Lenten resolution that Swinney once made.

"In all my years in the Church, that was a new one for me—to give up fear," the priest said. "I think we should all give up fear."

✠

Invitation/Challenge: To mark Good Friday one year, a high school offered a touching dramatization of the Stations of the Cross. As each Station was shared, a student portrayed one of the people who helped, watched or harmed Christ on the path to his crucifixion—Simon of Cyrene, Veronica, the women of Jerusalem, a Roman soldier, John the Apostle, the Blessed Mother. Each shared how interacting with Christ in his journey to his death moved them, and even changed them.

When the powerful presentation ended, the high school

students and adults who had been watching were invited to approach the full-size cross and attach their handwritten notes to Christ on it. The teenagers kept approaching the cross in waves. Many asked God to protect their friends and families. Some asked for forgiveness of their sins. Others asked for blessings for the poor, the homeless, the suffering and people who have lost loved ones. Then there were the more individual requests. One asked for prayers "for those who struggle with who they are." Another pleaded for "my dad's faith. He's falling away from God and his family, and it scares me." Another simply noted, "Help me."

By the time the last student affixed a plea, the wooden cross was transformed by the various colors of the notes: orange, blue, yellow, lime green and hot pink. Even more, the trust and hope of the students became attached to the cross—and the sacrifice it represents.

One of the great gifts of friendship comes when we reach a point where we realize we can't do something by ourselves, when we know that our burdens are too much to bear alone— and then a friend comes through for us, sharing the burden, lifting it from us. The greatest symbol of that gift of friendship is the cross. In accepting the agony of his crucifixion, Christ showed he would do anything to share our burdens, to lift them away for us.

If you had the opportunity, what message would you leave for Christ on the cross? What fear would you ask him to help you overcome?

Give up fear, knowing that you can leave it with God, knowing how much he loves you.

RISK LOSING SOMETHING THAT MATTERS TO YOU

The situation could have led to resentment and embarrassment—a situation where both sides could have walked away in disgust. Instead, it turned into a special story that touched people across the country because of its pure goodness.

The story began on an April afternoon as the freshman softball team of Roncalli High School prepared for a game against a team from John Marshall Community High School. At the time, the Roncalli team hadn't lost a game during its past two seasons. For the Marshall team, it was the first softball game in its high school's brief history.

As the girls from Marshall stepped off their bus and walked toward the field, Jeff Traylor—the junior varsity softball coach for Roncalli—was helping prepare the diamond. Before long, he started a conversation with one of the Marshall coaches, a conversation in which he learned that it was their first game ever, most of the girls had never previously played the sport, and they had only been practicing a short time—on a field that had trees growing in the outfield.

Looking at the Marshall players, Traylor noticed they didn't have cleats, sliding shorts, long socks or good gloves. He also saw that the inexperienced coaches weren't sure how to fill out the team's lineup card. So he helped them. Then he offered to stay in their dugout and answer any questions that the Marshall coaches had—an offer they accepted.

After one and a half innings of the game, it was clear that the contest was shaping up as a mismatch between a team that prides itself on a strong, winning tradition and a squad of inexperienced players who were just learning the game and wanted to be part of a team. Traylor arranged a conference between Marshall's coaches and the coaches of Roncalli's freshman team. They talked about stopping the game and spending the time instructing the Marshall players in the fundamentals of the sport. There was just one problem.

"The Marshall players did not want to quit," Traylor recalls. "They were willing to lose 100 to 0 if it meant they finished their first game."

To show their sincerity, Roncalli's freshman coaches, Sara Barna and Laura Laycock, offered to forfeit the game and still spend the time with the Marshall players—an offer from the team that hadn't lost in two years. That's when the Marshall players chose to forfeit the game.

"The Roncalli freshman team came over, introduced themselves and, with the Holy Spirit active in their hearts, took the field with the Marshall girls," Traylor notes. "They were practicing hitting, pitching and fielding. I could see the determination and a desire among the Marshall players to just be better. As they hit the ball, their faces lit up. They were high-fiving and hugging the girls from Roncalli, and thanking them for teaching them the game. They were having a blast."

Traylor was so moved by the interaction between the two teams that he sat down the next day and wrote an e-mail describing the experience to the parents of Roncalli's softball players and to the school's staff. Near the end of the e-mail, he wrote, "I tell all of you this story not only out of pride, but out of a sense that we can do more. I have some ideas of some great things we can do for these kids. I think every one of them deserves to have their own bats, gloves, cleats, sliders, batting helmets, all of it." Traylor then sent his message, never expecting what would happen next.

"The e-mail spread like a popular YouTube video," Traylor says. "I've gotten e-mails and phone calls from people all over the country. We've gotten massive amounts of equipment and monetary donations."

A few weeks later, the Roncalli freshman softball team invited the Marshall team back to Roncalli so they could practice together again. During the practice, the Marshall players received all the gloves, batting helmets and any other equipment they needed. But one of the true gifts of that beautiful, sunny afternoon was the attitude of the Marshall players.

"The Marshall players wanted to show us everything they had learned, and they wanted to learn more," Traylor says. "Their girls are so willing to learn."

They weren't the only ones who learned a lesson, Traylor believes.

"In sports, we're taught that winning is everything, and being the best is what's important. We're very strong as a program at Roncalli. We win a lot of games. But this time, it was bigger than winning, bigger than the game. Our girls knew that. It was more important for them to be there for another person and help them. The way everything has happened has been so moving for a lot of people, but for our girls it was so natural. They just saw it as what Jesus would have done."

Invitation/Challenge: We live in a world that seems to push us to turn inward, to focus on our own interests, to look past and even ignore the concerns that affect other people's lives. Reaching across the divides that supposedly separate us from other people involves risks. Our offers of grace, hope and friendship can leave us vulnerable, opening us to rejection and maybe even harm. And pride, fear and a feeling of unworthiness can prevent people from accepting our offers or making the most of them.

That's the way it is sometimes regarding what could be our most meaningful relationship. God reaches out to us, calling us to look beyond ourselves to a friendship that is more essential and life-giving: with him.

Cardinal Joseph Tobin talked about risk and the offer of a relationship with God in the advice he once gave to college students who were considering their futures.

"When you make your choice in life, you're taking the most

precious thing you have and betting on it," he said. "You're saying this is the way I think I will flourish as a man or a woman. Think about what would make you holy, what would help you belong, what's worth risking your life for."

He then referred to a point in John's Gospel where two disciples follow Jesus, and Jesus turns and asks, "What are you looking for?" (John 1:38)

Cardinal Tobin said to the college students, "Jesus asks you and me, 'What are you looking for? What do you think you need? What do you want to be? What will make you happy and whole?' "

They're soul-searching questions, ones that close friends could naturally ask each other. And the best answers to these questions, Cardinal Tobin said, can be found in the example of Jesus who lived his life and sacrificed his life for others.

"Jesus is not a hopeless victim," he told the college students. "He chooses. He made the supreme gesture of liberty—giving his life away. Whatever particular vocation we ultimately say yes to in this life, we say yes in order that God may live in us and send us out, broken and poured out, for the life of the world."

The life of the world always grows stronger when we reach across the divides, when we reach out to each other. Just ask the players on two special softball teams.

Risk losing something that is important to you—a certain victory, your pride, *yourself*—in the hope of gaining a closer relationship with others and with God.

KEEP THE PROMISE

As the mirrored ball created a sky of swirling stars in the roller-skating rink, everyone's eyes turned to the unusual couple among them. Stooped and gray-haired, the man used his burned stump of a left hand to help him push his wheelchair-bound, seemingly comatose wife around the glossy wooden floor. Smiling, the man occasionally wiggled the chair to the music, as if they were dancing.

None of the other skaters recognized that the man is one of the most successful drivers in the history of motor sports—a former racer at the Indianapolis 500 and a 10-time national champion. None of the other skaters knew that the woman was once an accomplished painter and sculptor. And none of the other skaters realized they were witnessing one of the last hauntingly beautiful chapters of a great love story—the story of a couple that started at this skating rink long ago.

Mel Kenyon was 30 in 1963, a man who enjoyed gliding around roller-skating rinks when he wasn't roaring around race tracks. After lacing up his skates that day, the young race car driver took the floor when the rink manager announced it was time for a "bell skate." Males and females suddenly became pairs around the floor, and every time the manager rang a bell, each guy would separate from his partner and join the female ahead of him. That's how Mel met Marieanne. Wearing slacks and a sweater, the blonde, blue-eyed farmer's daughter stood 5 feet, 9 inches—an inch taller than Mel. Yet something else about the beautiful 20-year-old stood out to him as they circled the floor together.

"She smelled good," Mel recalls, smiling.

He had to let her skate with other guys as the bell skate continued, but when it ended, he sped to her side. They fox-trotted, two-stepped and waltzed together on skates that night. A week later, he asked her to a movie. Smitten, he was confident she was the one, but he had to know for sure. So he put her to his ultimate test. He asked her to one of his races.

She enjoyed it. Six months later, they were engaged. A year later, they were married. Then came the incident that Mel calls "the bonfire"—a racing accident that nearly killed him and instead changed his life and his relationship with Marieanne forever.

The bonfire erupted at the Langhorne race track in Pennsylvania in June 1965. On the 27th lap, Kenyon's car spun after blowing its engine, bounced off the wall and came to a complete stop. The impact left him unconscious. Even worse, the two racers behind him—who were involved in a fierce battle for position—never saw his stopped car until it was too late. They both rammed into Kenyon's car, which still had 65 gallons of fuel in the tank. His car exploded into flames as it skidded across the infield.

"Joe Leonard, the national champion from the year before, saw what was happening, pulled into the infield, got out of the car and came to my aid. Two other guys helped him," Kenyon recalls. "By the time a jeep got there with fire bottles, I was in the fire for three minutes."

He had third-degree burns—the worst—on 40 percent of his body, including his face, chest and both legs. His left hand was burned to a stump.

"Marieanne got one of those phone calls a wife never wants to get," he says. "We had been married only a year and two months. When she saw me, she didn't recognize me. I was all wrapped up (in bandages) from head to foot, like a mummy. They had to put my nose back on, rearrange my face. There were 17 operations. We didn't have any kids yet, so I was her first baby. She fed me and did everything for me for a month."

Marieanne also did something for him that changed his life.

"She had been working on me all the time to find the Lord, but until the burn center it didn't happen. With Marieanne's help, I turned over what was left of my miserable life to the

Lord Jesus—for him to do with me what he wanted, not what I wanted. Twelve doctors said I'd be in the burn center for nine months or better. With the Lord's help and healing, I was ready to leave two weeks after I gave my life to him. In all, it was three months instead of nine months."

While the accident brought Mel closer to God, it brought him and Marieanne even closer as a couple. Mel returned to racing in February 1966, using a prosthesis on his left hand to help him steer. With Marieanne by his side, he began a comeback that would lead him to his first appearance in the Indianapolis 500 that same year. Mel finished fifth in the 1966 500-Mile Race—one of the eight races he would run at the Speedway, one of his four top-five finishes there.

At every turn, Marieanne admired the way Mel approached each race with a desire to push himself and his car to the limit. He admired her ability as an artist, her approach to teaching disabled children to swim, the way she was willing to tackle anything.

"She was a racing fan, and she helped me with the race car," he says. "When I was injured in 1969 in Michigan after smacking the wall, she fashioned up a crutch for me. I directed her to take apart the bent race car so we could fix it. She was pregnant with Vaughn at the time."

Vaughn was born, then Brice arrived two years later. By then, Mel's driving career centered on racing midget cars. The family of four followed the midget racing tour through the United States during the summer, and New Zealand and Australia during the winter. There was plenty of reason to smile and celebrate as Mel continued to pile up the victories and the national championships.

"He was almost unbeatable with those cars," recalls Vaughn Kenyon. "As for my mom, she used to do the portraits of the Indianapolis 500 winners. And she was right there with every aspect of our childhood. It was all a lot of fun. We did most everything together as a family."

In 1991, the family was looking forward to Mel competing in the first annual Mel Kenyon Classic, a race established in his honor at Indianapolis Raceway Park. Yet the day before that inaugural race, an accident again changed the Kenyons' lives. This time, it happened to Marieanne.

An avid bicycle rider, Marieanne routinely rode 15 to 20 miles each morning before she went to work. On that August morning in 1991, Mel realized she was late getting home, but he didn't make any connection when an ambulance's siren wailed past their house.

"An airline flight controller who lives nearby saw it all," Mel says. "It happened about a half-mile from our house. She was coming home when a neighbor's dog ran right at her bike. She always took a squirt gun with ammonia in it for that purpose. But this time, she didn't have the squirt gun with her. Evidently, she put the brakes on, but she couldn't stop. When the wheel turned, the bike dumped her and slammed her head against the pavement. Her body rolled over, but her head stayed, twisting her spinal cord and neck."

Her bicycle helmet had been of little benefit. She was rushed by helicopter to a hospital. Mel rushed to see her. The doctors told him the injury was on the right side of her head, the same place she had been injured in a bike accident three years earlier. Mel stayed by her side, touched her and thought about the 10 times he had been knocked unconscious while driving a race car, the 10 times he had always recovered mentally. He prayed that God would spare her, too.

It wasn't to be.

"She couldn't walk, talk or move," he says. "After six months, I had an MRI done on her. They said there was no hope ever of recovery."

People told Mel he should put her in a nursing home, that her care would be too demanding, that he should get on with his life. But the memory of the Langhorne accident, his painful stay in the burn center and Marieanne's devotion to him were etched in his soul. He knew he could never walk away from her.

When he raced, he would take her to a nursing home so she would have someone to care for her while he was away. But when the races ended, he always took her home to care for her. He pushed her wheelchair through the house, taking her into the studio where she had loved to sculpt figures and paint portraits. He also took her with him when he had speaking engagements around the country and the world. Churches and Christian groups wanted to hear his inspirational story of finding Christ, of not losing hope when tragedy strikes—a talk that Mel calls, "The Sudden Stops in Life."

"You never know when the sudden stops are going to happen, but they will happen," he says. "Like my bonfire, like Marieanne's bike accident. So having the Lord on your side prior to the sudden stops makes it a whole lot easier to accept, adjust and overcome."

When people saw Marieanne at those talks or when Mel led her around the roller-skating rink, they saw a woman who seemed unresponsive to life, unresponsive to others. Having looked closer than anyone else, Mel viewed Marieanne differently. He saw how she was able to move her left leg and her left foot to music. He saw how she followed a conversation, how she talked with her eyes—one blink for "no" and several for "yes." He noticed how the visits to the roller rink seemed to be as good for her as they were for him.

Like skating rinks and race tracks, our lives often come full circle, leading us back to our starting points. After a race in Ohio in December, Mel returned home. Keeping with tradition, he planned to take Marieanne to her parents' house in Illinois a week before Christmas. The plan also called for their annual visit to the Illinois roller-skating rink where they first met—to let all the years and all the sudden stops of their lives fade for a while.

They never made the trip. Two days before their planned departure, Mel woke up next to Marieanne, not realizing her life was about to end.

"I cleaned her up, then I got back into bed with her," he recalls, closing his eyes, trying to keep the tears inside. "We held hands. I told her how good she was doing and wished her the Lord's blessing. Then we went back to sleep. I woke up to feed her at 8:30, but she was already gone."

His tears flow easily as he talks about how she died by his side, how he bathed his wife, washed her hair and dressed her before taking her to the funeral home. His tears continue as he talks about how caring for Marieanne for the past eight years and four months was never a burden to him.

"The Lord loves us, and we're to love our mate through thickness and thin," he says. "It was just a pleasure doing it for her because she had done it for me. It was just love."

Just love. A love as timeless as two people holding onto each other and staying by each other as the years kept coming round and round.

✠

Invitation/Challenge: We make promises all through our lives—to our parents, our friends, our spouse, our children. When we make promises, we are offering more than a pledge or a vow. We are offering the best of ourselves. While most promises are made to another person, there are also the promises we make to ourselves, and the promises we make to God.

In the 50th year of his priesthood, Father Theodore Hesburgh, the late president of the University of Notre Dame, shared with me the pledge he made to God when he was ordained on June 24, 1943. He promised to celebrate a Mass every day of his life, "even though the Church did not require that of me or any other priest."

"I felt the greatest thing you can do as a priest is to offer Mass," he said. "So I felt if that's the greatest privilege I have, I didn't want to waste it. I've been able to do it every day for 50 years with the exception of two or three times."

He then shared the story of one of those exceptions, when he was helping keep vigil during the birth of a baby. It was a day when he had been pacing the maternity ward for hours, smoking cigarette after cigarette with the expectant father, when he saw a nurse rush from the delivery room with the baby. The baby had been born prematurely, weighed about three pounds, and was struggling for his life.

"The nurse went tearing up the steps, and we tore after her," he recalled. "It turns out the baby wasn't breathing, and the nurse was taking him up to the oxygen tank on the next floor. She turned it on, put the baby's face in the mask, and it didn't work.

"I asked if the baby still had a heartbeat, and the nurse said, 'Yes.' I said to the father, 'We'd better baptize him. What do you want to call him?' He said, 'Mark.' We went over to the sink. The water was very cold, and when I sloshed it on the kid and baptized him, he let out a monumental yell. That's how he started breathing."

Father Ted's face glowed as he told that story. The smile remained as he shared how that baby had grown up to be a 48-year-old man who had just sent him a note congratulating him on his 50th anniversary as a priest.

His smile then turned to a laugh as he recalled a humorous story concerning his promise to celebrate Mass every day—a story about the unlikely encounter he had during a trip that had him traveling from the United States to Rome to Jerusalem, all in one day.

Realizing that the only chance he had to celebrate Mass that day was during a stopover in Rome, Father Ted rushed to a small, seedy hotel near the airport. When he asked the hotel's owner for a room for just one hour, she looked at him suspiciously.

Father Ted recalled with a laugh, "I told her if she had any bad thoughts about it, she could come up and watch me offer Mass. When I came down to pay the bill, she said, 'No, you have sanctified my hotel.'" With another laugh, Father Ted said he told her, "It sure needs it."

In those two stories from Father Hesburgh, we are shown two realities about the promises we make. Sometimes, extraordinary circumstances arise that take priority over the promise we made. And sometimes it takes extraordinary measures to live up to our promise. Both realities show the extreme importance of the promises we make. They constantly call us to sacrifice our self-interest, to give the best of ourselves, to live life for others. Christ willingly made—and kept—that promise to God and us.

What are the promises you have made to give the best of yourself?

Keep the promise.

TAKE A LEAP OF FAITH

After 15 failed attempts at making his dream come true, Tim Hahn knew he was down to two very different choices. He could give up the dream, even though that would mean going against his whole approach to life since he was a boy—to keep fighting to beat the odds. So Hahn considered his other choice as he stood outside the grocery market.

In the previous few weeks, he had already been to 15 grocery stores in the city, hoping to get a store manager to agree to donate surplus food so that he could fulfill his wish to help feed the poor. Yet Hahn had been turned down every time.

"I realized I'm not a good salesman," he recalls. "I stood out in front of that store knowing it's my last chance and thinking it's not going to work. I said, 'Jesus, I'm obviously doing something wrong. So I'm just going to move my lips and let you do the talking.' I went in the store and that's exactly what happened. I talked to the manager, and within 60 seconds he's nodding his head."

Still amazed by that moment, Hahn pauses before he adds, "I think Jesus is so grateful when people help other people. I think he just says, 'Of course, I'll help. Just get out of the way.' I've learned to get out of the way. I've learned to take the leap of faith."

With that approach, Hahn has built a grassroots, non-profit organization called Helping Hand, a volunteer effort that provides food for the predominantly Hispanic families who live near his home. And every step of the way has led to another story that has shown him the value of the adage, "Let go, and let God." Just consider the story of how he found the site where he would give food to the poor, and how he found the people he believes that he was destined to help.

He and his wife, Linda, were driving to a produce stand

shortly after he had received the unexpected blessing from the store manager. That's when Hahn saw a grassy area and a parking lot that he thought would be a perfect site for distributing the food.

"It was right next to this roadhouse bar," he recalls. "I told my wife, 'That's where we're going to set up the stand.' She didn't say anything so I know she didn't agree with me. I stopped and went in the bar. It's a rough place. I talked to the woman behind the bar and told her I wanted to give away food in the parking lot on Saturdays. She looked at me, walked away and waited on three more customers. Then she came back and said, 'What did you say?'

"I told her and added, 'I know you open at noon, and I'll be gone by then.' She walked away again and waited on three more people. She came back again, and she was wringing her hands with this towel. She said, 'You know, that's the best idea I've heard all day. OK.'

"I turned around and this guy stood up. He was six-foot-six so it took him a while. He said, 'What are you going to do?' I said, 'I'm going to give away food in that parking lot. You want to help?' He gave me five bucks—my first tithe—and he pointed to a trailer behind the bar and said, 'That lady broke her leg. She probably needs help.' I saw all the other trailers there, and knew that's where the poor were. We showed up the next week."

While Hahn's leaps of faith have led him to moments that have made him soar, he has also had a few difficult landings. One notable situation occurred three months after he started his effort. As nearly 90 people lined up for food on a Saturday morning that began in gorgeous sunshine, Hahn noticed a group of men who stood away from the crowd, watching the scene. He figured the men had relatives in line, but they felt awkward about seeing their families receive help. Soon, he was distracted by a young boy and an older woman who had problems that couldn't be solved with a bag of groceries. His growing frustration overflowed when it started raining.

"It was depressing to me," he recalls. "I looked over toward where the men had been standing and they were gone. I thought, 'Thanks a lot.' We tried to protect ourselves and the food as best we could, but it wasn't working. I was mad at God for making it rain on me. Then the men who had been standing away reappeared with a big, plastic sheet, and they held it up while everyone else went through the line. I responded with a one-word prayer to God: 'Sorry.' "

The moment reinforced for Hahn that leaps of faith are held up by wings of trust.

Hahn took another leap of faith after he received an e-mail from a teacher who shared the stunning reality of one of her students, a teenager with special needs, including autism.

"He came to school and began to cry in front of her," Hahn recalls. "When asked why he was so sad, he said he didn't have a bed. Never has. He's 15. He thought maybe lots of kids didn't, but as he spent time at friends' houses, he saw most kids do. But not him. She asked for help."

So Hahn went to his organization's storage shed and found an old, donated mattress. But after looking at it, he decided to take a different approach. He went shopping to buy the youth a new mattress, frame and box springs. At the first mattress store he visited, he shared the story of the youth and asked for a price. When he thought it was too high, he visited a second store, shared the teenager's story again, and this time the salesperson gave him a price nearly below cost. Hahn paid for the bed. That day, he also paid a light bill and two partial rents for people in need—a total cost of $800.

Still, Hahn felt good in his heart when he went out to dinner that same day with his wife and friends. In the middle of the dinner, he received a phone call from a number he didn't recognize. He excused himself to take the call, heading outside the restaurant.

"This young woman said, 'Are you Tim Hahn?' " he recalls. "She said, 'I work at a boutique store. I heard what you do, and we'd like to help. We want to give you 10 percent of our profits on Mondays for two months.' This would be leading up to Christmas, so I asked her, 'How much do you think that would be?' She said, 'About $4,000.' "

Looking back on all the events of that day, Hahn shares his philosophy about giving: "Whenever you take a little leap of faith, God won't be outdone in his generosity. That always happens."

⁜

Invitation/Challenge: In thinking about my friendships, there's not many where I can pinpoint the exact circumstances when our bond began. Most of them evolved over time, until they reached a point where the connections just flowed naturally. Yet I'll never forget the moment when my friendship with Joe Wilson started. Just seconds after I met Joe for the first time, the Irish singer and musician made me an unusual and generous offer. He made the offer before I even settled into a chair inside his house, where I had come to interview him as a writer. The mischief danced in Joe's eyes as he leaned toward me and said, "I have a fine bottle of Irish whiskey that can't be bought here in the States. And it's the last bottle I have. Would you like a drink?"

Before I could answer, Joe winked and whispered, "Of course, once we take off the cork, we throw it away."

As I considered the offer to savor and empty a bottle of fine Irish whiskey with Joe, I also imagined the condition I would be in if I accepted his offer. I would have to explain to my family, my bosses and the police that the reason I was missing for two days was because I had spent that time passed out in Joe's music room.

That image made me politely decline Joe's offer. Yet even though I didn't accept his offer, I did take away something far more lasting. I mean, here was someone I had never met before, and within minutes he was offering me the best he had to give.

Since we are all made in the image and likeness of God, I like to think there is a glimpse of God in the best qualities of my friends. I see a hint of God's generosity in Joe Wilson. There are also glimpses of God in a friend who exudes a quiet strength, in another friend who models goodness and grace, and in another friend who has always seemed to look beyond my faults, who constantly welcomes me with joy, and continues to see the best in me. I also like to think there is a glimpse of God in the laughter I share with my friends and in the heartaches we share.

In many ways, a friendship requires a leap of faith. In opening ourselves to another person, we leave ourselves vulnerable to being rejected, to being hurt, to having our trust betrayed. In opening ourselves to a friendship with God, we also leave ourselves vulnerable—to letting go of trying to control our lives, and instead putting our trust in God. In both types of friendships, the rewards are worth the leap of faith. Joe Wilson offered the best he had—in his life, in his friendships. And yet it's just a glimpse of the generosity that God offers us. As Tim Hahn says, "Whenever you take a little leap of faith, God won't be outdone in his generosity."

Take the leap of faith.

RISE AND SOAR

(This essay was written by Kathleen Shaughnessy, my daughter, before her senior year in college.)

There is a park five minutes from my house. On the corner, close to the trail that runners, rollerbladers and bikers occupy on summer days, one can find my favorite place in the park—the swing set. I love the feeling of the wind whispering through my hair as my legs gradually start to sway back and forth, back and forth. As my momentum builds, a smile sweeps across my face. Like a bird discovering how to use its wings, I begin to fly. And for that brief moment at the top of my swing, I feel untouchable. However, one second later, my stomach will inevitably drop, and I will ricochet back to where I started, ready to begin the adventure all over again.

In many ways, my life has been like the swing set I love so much. I began my most recent adventure three years ago when I took my first steps onto the University of Notre Dame's campus as a student. In the August heat, my legs began to pump, trying out clubs and making new friends. I felt my momentum starting to build. And just when I reached the top of the swing's arc, a horrible, uneasy feeling overwhelmed me. "I don't belong here," I mumbled through the tears running down my cheeks. My sense of self that had been derived from high school accomplishments seemed underwhelming in comparison with the people surrounding me. I remember thinking that everyone was so talented. I struggled to acknowledge what I brought to the table. It was only when I spoke with my "big sister" Lauren that my legs began to pump once again.

Using Mother Teresa's words to refuel me, Lauren said: "When we have nothing to give, let us give Him that nothingness. Let us remain as empty as possible, so that God can fill us… Take away your eyes from yourself and rejoice that you have nothing… Give Jesus a big smile every time your nothingness scares you."

As hard as it was, I woke up every day trying to see my nothingness as a blessing. I centered myself on letting the Lord fill me through the stories of others, whether it was the people I met at the medical clinic where I volunteered, my friends down the hallway, or the third graders I mentored at Take Ten, a violence prevention program, or Girls on the Run, a girls' empowerment program. By the time I returned to the top of the swing, I was ready for a bigger service role.

I applied for and was awarded a grant to work with the underserved populations of a Midwestern city. As I served at Matthew 25, a health and dental clinic, the feeling of uneasiness became a daily occurrence. I encountered domestic abuse victims, homeless men struggling to find work, and immigrants fighting to adjust to life in America. I constantly questioned why God had blessed me with the life I have when others were struggling to meet such basic needs. But as my time at Matthew 25 progressed, my legs found their power once more.

As a medical aide and an assistant to a physical therapist, I learned something from each of the patients I helped. One woman didn't want me to make the same mistakes she made in a relationship. After recounting the story of her husband's domestic abuse, she whispered, "Just make sure he is the right one, ok, honey?" A man taught me the importance of forgiveness. "I'm going to do better. This time will be different. My family is there to support me." He had just been released from jail. Another person kept me grounded. "Even with a busy schedule, never forget to love. That's the only thing you will leave behind when you are gone. She just didn't have enough time." Her 43-year-old daughter had died just months ago.

Listening to the people's stories and acknowledging their hardships prepared me for my study abroad experience in Santiago, Chile. Here the roles would be reversed, and I would be the outcast. One day, I stood in Teletón, an organization that provides free physical therapy to children in Chile with neurological disorders, and the place where I did service once a week. On that day, I felt defeated as I listened to the therapists laugh over my various mess-ups. "She doesn't understand a thing we say," I heard them mock in Spanish. I knew enough Spanish to understand.

I left the clinic that day sniffling back tears. I waited at the bus station for my friend, Becky, and when she arrived, I melted into her arms, my tears staining her shirt. As she tried to make sense of my story through my sobbing, we were interrupted by a Chilean drag queen: "Don't cry over him, honey. You are too beautiful to cry over a boy." I couldn't help it, I burst out laughing. He misunderstood the situation, but his humanity saved me. It also gave me the encouragement to continue speaking Spanish. I made progress little by little, reaching the point where I had the ability to communicate fluently with the people I served this summer in Guatemala, teaching in a school and working in a medical clinic.

I think it's safe to say that I have reached the top of the swing arc once again. Even though I know that means more bumps lie ahead of me, I don't mind. I know now that the worst I can have is nothing, and as Mother Teresa says, that's not such a bad thing after all.

✠

Invitation/Challenge: I have a friend who can vividly remember scenes—and quote lines—years later from his favorite television show. I have no such talent, being someone who often forgets why I just went into another room to get something. Still, there is one episode from a short-lived, futuristic television series that has stayed in my mind for years.

If my memory serves me well about this episode, the punishment for people who break the law in this futuristic society requires them to wear an imbedded symbol on their forehead. They still have their freedom to live among other people in society, but their punishment involves being forbidden to interact with anyone, touch anyone or talk to anyone. If they do, the length of their sentence increases. And if anyone in society ignores the incriminating symbol on their forehead and reaches out to them in any way, that person suffers the same fate and punishment.

In the course of the episode, a law-breaker is shown suffering from the effects of that punishment. Even though he is "free" to live in the society, the results of the loss of his interaction with other people devastate him. Still, he serves his sentence, and the imbedded symbol is removed. Once again, he is immersed among people who acknowledge him, touch him and interact with him. And the change in him is transformative. He's happy, connected, whole again. Yet the climatic scene shows the true transformation in him. It comes when he sees a law-breaker over the course of a few days, a law-breaker suffering from the same soul-robbing punishment of being personally disconnected from other people. All that pain, all that loss returns to the man's face again as he watches the despairing woman. And the episode ends with the man walking up to her and embracing her as guards rush toward both of them.

That moment is the essence of compassion—a quality that always seems to deepen the level of our friendships and our humanity. Indeed, compassion may be the most hard-earned human quality we learn because we've had to suffer to attain it. Yet through our own heartbreak, we are far more able to acknowledge, understand and help heal the heartbreak that other people endure. In the situation of my daughter, a friend who has experienced emptiness herself shares the wisdom of a saint. Older people who have made mistakes and have suffered loss provide thoughtful advice. A stranger who has known rejection and ridicule offers comfort and concern. And through the help of these people who have experienced despair, rejection and ridicule, a person rises from these depths herself and soars toward a higher level of purpose, humility and humanity.

That quality of compassion is also at the heart of God's relationship with us. Our only path to him is through his mercy and compassion. So he shows his love for us by sending his son to live among us, to suffer for us, to die for us. And amid his excruciating suffering and death—a time of despair, ridicule and rejection—Jesus says, "Father, forgive them, for they know not what they do." In that moment, compassion is revealed at its highest human and divine level. In that moment, we are offered a soul-stirring example of the way we should respond to others in need of compassion.

Be the person who helps others rise from their depths to soar. Be the person who rises from the depths and soars.

MAKE TIME

The page came at 10 minutes before midnight, calling Father John Mannion to the hospital room of the dying woman. Entering the room, Father Mannion realized he had never met the woman or her 80-year-old husband who sat by her side, praying that their marriage of 40 years wasn't coming to an end.

Father Mannion administered last rites to Rita Ressler. And when she died minutes later, the priest tried to comfort her husband, Charlie, as he whimpered, "I lost my Rita. I lost my Rita. What am I going to do?" After Charlie mentioned they had no children, he looked into the eyes of the priest and asked, "Will you help take care of me?"

That question led to a promise—and the beginning of a remarkable relationship between Charlie and Father Mannion, the director of spiritual care services at St. Francis Hospital. Since that moment eight years ago, Father Mannion has spent a part of nearly every day taking care of Charlie—a connection that continued as the 64-year-old priest drove to see his friend who lives in a Catholic hermitage.

"After Rita died, he would always be at the hospital every night after work—faithfully," Father Mannion recalled. "He'd be sitting here at my desk or he'd wait on a bench until I came to the door. I'd go over to his house every night and talk to him for an hour or so. He was so lonely. For the past three years, since he's been at the hermitage, I've gone every day, seven days a week, two times a day."

As he talked, Father Mannion drove his pickup truck, having lent his car for the week to a couple whose vehicle was in the shop to fix its transmission. The drive to the hermitage recalled his days as a parish priest when he made unusual, extra deliveries as he distributed Holy Communion to the parish's shut-ins every Friday. On those days, Father Mannion also brought each of the shut-ins at the small, rural parish their favorite dessert—having spent the previous night cooking in his kitchen, making cinnamon rolls, chocolate cake, and lemon, cherry and apple pies.

The drive to the hermitage also recalled a day from two years ago when he nearly bled to death. On that day, he had been fixing the power mower of a former neighbor—an act of kindness similar to the way he paints houses and cleans gutters for people in need.

"I had my hand under the mower and my left hand went into the sharpened blade," he recalled. "It severely cut my thumb halfway around. I drove to St. Francis with a floorboard filled with blood. When I got there, I told the doctor I was tired. The doctor said, 'Sure, you're tired. You left half your blood in the truck.' "

After parking at the hermitage, Father Mannion walked inside, where he saw Charlie sitting in his wheelchair with his back to the priest. Father Mannion sneaked toward Charlie and put his hands on his friend's arms. When the priest came in front of Charlie, Charlie smiled. As the two friends talked, Father Mannion gave Charlie his full attention. The priest never gave an indication that he supervises a staff of 21 people, chairs the hospital's institutional ethics committee, and reviews hardship cases for employees. It's a 24-hour, 7-day-a-week job, but he still makes time for Charlie.

It's a quality he said he learned from his father.

"When I was ordained, my father, being of Irish descent, was proud," said Father Mannion, one of seven children. "On my ordination, he said, 'There are three 'L's' to life, and I never want you to forget them: Live, love and learn.' Then my dad said to me, 'You know, son, if you combine all three of those, life is always sacred.'

"That has really been my whole priesthood. In order to live, you have to be alive to the moment. To love is the fulfillment of the Gospel. Can you do it for someone else? And to learn is to always be open for growth and change, to always see life as a new beginning."

Charlie knows that Father Mannion has offered him a new beginning.

"We're good friends," Charlie said as Father Mannion left his room to get him a cup of ice cream. "I see him every day, every evening."

Charlie counts on Father Mannion so much that when the priest had back surgery and couldn't come to visit him, Charlie kept calling people until someone gave him a ride to Father Mannion's home.

"It's a very deep, very loving relationship," said LaRena Brown, Father Mannion's office manager. "My concern for John is that he thinks so much of Charlie, he doesn't think of himself. He's a giver."

That description is the ultimate compliment to the priest. Even as he said goodbye to Charlie after lunch, he promised to return in the evening to cook dinner for him—"We're having bacon and macaroni and cheese tonight, Charlie"—just as he always does.

"I put him to bed every night," Father Mannion said. "When I put him to bed, I always say, 'I love you, Charlie.' I started that about three years ago because I'm not sure he'll be there tomorrow when I come."

Father Mannion never expected a response to his nightly expression of love. After all, Charlie comes from the same generation of males as the priest's father, men who have always expressed their love in their actions and their sacrifices rather than their words.

Yet months ago, Charlie said something that made the priest smile.

"I put him to bed and said, 'I love you, Charlie.' His response was a low, 'Me, too.' About three or four days later, I said, 'I love you, Charlie.' He said, 'You know that I love you, too.' "

Father Mannion smiled as he told that story. His expression didn't change when he was asked about his dedication to Charlie and whether the eight years—and counting—of daily visits have been worth his time.

"I would do it all over again," he said. "I wouldn't question one second. It's like my father said, 'Whatever talents God gives you in life, give them away.' He always felt that in giving, we receive. I feel Charlie has given me more than I ever gave him."

✠

Invitation/Challenge: At its heart, a relationship with God begins as an invitation—an invitation to talk with God, move closer to him, and live our lives in a Christ-like way that will lead us to join him in heaven. That invitation is unique in another way, too. It's marked by challenges that test our hearts and our souls to our human limits: Pick up your cross, turn the other cheek, forgive 70 times 7, believe without seeing, love your neighbor as yourself, "not as I will, but as you will."

In today's world, another challenge seems just as daunting: Make time.

Everything in our lives today seems designed to save us time or to maximize the way we use our time. Yet so many of us feel we don't have enough time. There are work demands, school demands, laundry demands, food shopping demands, car pool demands, house upkeep demands—so many demands that erode the time we have for ourselves, and limit our desire to be more of a presence in the lives of others. Christ understands that challenge. In his three years of building a team, teaching, healing, traveling, public speaking, dealing with doubters, fending off enemies, and trying to spread a message the world had never heard—all while striving to be a presence to family and friends—Christ knew the limits of time.

He also knew the importance, and the rewards, of making time. As he once raced to the next thing on his list, he felt someone reach out to touch his cloak. So he stopped and listened. When he heard a friend was in need, he changed his plans to be there for his friend. Even when he was being betrayed in the Garden of Gethsemane, he paused to heal the ear of one of his captors. The person before him always mattered. He stopped or slowed down. He listened and healed—with words or deeds. He made time.

For Father Mannion, it comes down to a belief and a question, "In order to live, you have to be alive to the moment. To love is the fulfillment of the Gospel. Can you do it for someone else?" Can you do it for your friendship with God?

Make time.

FIND YOUR WAY BACK TO GOD

Michael Walterman will always remember his 18th birthday for two life-changing reasons. First, it was the day when one of his best friends committed suicide. And, because of that death, it was also the day when he turned his back on God.

"I wanted no part of a God who would allow these types of things to happen," Walterman recalls. "I couldn't understand. I basically gave up on God."

A few moments later, he adds, "Years later, I would discover that God never gave up on me."

Those two polar-opposite revelations hint at the profound, deeply personal story of Walterman's return to faith. It's a story marked by two devastating realities in his life—the suicide of one of his best friends and the heartbreak of what happened to Walterman's mother. After the suicide of his friend, Walterman stopped going to Mass and gave up on his plans to receive the sacrament of confirmation.

"After abandoning God, things became increasingly difficult for me," he says. "I went to college, but with more trouble than success. I also battled depression."

Dropping out of college, he saw "a cycle of depression, loneliness and separation from God" continue for years until his mother sat down with him one night and told him that he needed God in his life.

"She was crying for me and made me promise that I would start going to Mass again at least once a month. I obliged her and said that I would. But I didn't keep my promise—at least not until she got sick. On Mother's Day, my mom sat my brothers and I down and told us she had kidney cancer."

The heartbreak continued when she also experienced early dementia, which led the family to admit her to a nursing home for in-patient care.

"While my family and I went through this nightmare, I started thinking more and more that I should go back to Mass. By this point, I realized I really did believe in God after all, and he was good—ironic, considering a lot of people in my position would have blamed God for such heartache. But I did not. In fact, my faith started to grow. But I didn't quite have the strength to go back to church just yet. I guess I was afraid I wouldn't belong anymore or it wouldn't feel right. I just didn't have the courage yet. That is until one morning when I experienced something. It was the most amazing moment of my life."

On a Sunday morning, Walterman believes God spoke to him, telling him, "Mike, it's time to go back to church." Walterman acknowledges that many people would say he's "crazy" to think he heard the voice of God, but he also insists, "I truly believe that God was speaking to me." That Sunday, he headed to a nearby church. He was surprised and appreciated that several people warmly greeted him—a stranger—as he sat near the back of the church. He was also surprised that the celebration of the Mass left him "filled with joy and relief and hope."

Feeling a change within him, he decided to receive the sacrament of confirmation at Easter that year. He just hoped that his mother could be there.

He recalls that Easter as "one of the happiest days of my life." As he was confirmed, he was surrounded by his father, his brothers, other relatives and friends. But it was also a bittersweet day. His mother was too ill to attend.

"In the weeks leading up to Easter, her condition was worsening steadily. But there were still plenty of times when she would be coherent and alert when I would visit her. I would bring her figurines of angels and tell her all about going back to Mass and going through confirmation."

Walterman believes those moments helped his mother find "a little peace in knowing that my soul was healing." He also believes that one of the reasons God led him to return to the Church was to give him strength and faith during his mother's illness. He said he needed that strength and faith when his mother died on the day after Mother's Day.

"At her funeral, I put a trinket in her blouse pocket. It was a little key—St. Peter's key to the gates of heaven, though she did not need it. I put it there as a reminder that she was my key to heaven. I don't claim to know or understand God's plan, but I do know that if it weren't for her, I would have never found my faith again."

As Walterman looks back on the transformation of his life, he sees it as a story of faith, joy and renewal for others who have separated from God.

"I feel that if God could change my heart and bring me back to the Church, then he could do it for anyone. If you are depressed or lost or lonely or confused or hopeless, just remember that even if you have lost your faith in God, he still has faith in you. You're never too far gone for God to find you."

Invitation/Challenge: It's the only time in my life when I wished I had a can of spray paint so I could add to the graffiti that someone had scrawled in the midst of a major city. Spray-painted in white, the large one-word statement appeared suddenly as I walked along the busy streets of Chicago near Wrigley Field. I had just savored a glorious summer afternoon of baseball, but my thoughts shifted when I saw the word near the curb of a sidewalk:

FORGIVE.

It's an invitation and a challenge that gets you thinking, and my thoughts immediately turned to a few specific moments in my life when I had been hurt by someone, when the pain and rejection I felt seared into my heart and my soul. I also remember how I held onto that pain and rejection, finding it difficult to forgive the people who I felt had let me down or done me wrong. Fortunately, the years have passed since those moments, the pain and rejection have faded, and I've made peace with those people, sometimes in person and other times in my heart.

In the midst of remembering those moments when I needed to forgive, I had the sudden wish to be holding a can of white spray paint. With the word FORGIVE emblazoned in my mind, I wanted to change the original message on that sidewalk by adding seven letters to it. And so I imagined myself using the spray paint to make an A, followed by an S, followed by a K. Then I saw myself adding four more letters to the end of FORGIVE, the suffix NESS. So when I was done with my imaginary spray-painting, the message on the street would declare to people passing by, ASK FORGIVENESS.

Maybe it's the type of person I am, but in matters of mercy *to ask forgiveness* is the second hardest part for me. I know my faults, I know my mistakes, I know the times when I hurt people, but I have sometimes struggled to verbalize such failings—to simply say, 'I'm sorry I have hurt you. Can you forgive me?" And yet when I have sought forgiveness, it has usually moved me closer to the people I have offended. Still, when I look back across my life, I think of people I have hurt, people to whom I didn't acknowledge my failure of love and friendship, people who—because of distances and circumstances that can't be overcome now—I am not able to seek their forgiveness. So I make my confession to God, ask forgiveness from him and promise to treat others better. That reality, that regret, that promise also leads me to want to reach for the can of white spray paint again, to alter once more the original message, FORGIVE—this time to what is often the hardest part of forgiveness for me and many other people.

And so I imagine myself adding an eight-letter word after FORGIVE, spray-painting a Y, followed by an O, an U, an R, an S, an E, an L and an F, so the message now reads, FORGIVE YOURSELF.

We often let our mistakes and our weaknesses haunt us. We often fail to remember that we are human, and that means we will never be perfect. We often forget to realize that in admitting our weaknesses and striving to change them, we open ourselves to strengthening our relationships with other people and with God. The process begins with forgiving ourselves, a process that should be easier to embrace knowing that God is always willing to forgive us—if we just ask.

So there's the trinity of forgiveness: forgive, ask forgiveness and forgive yourself. Admittedly, together they would make for a crowded message spray-painted on a busy city street. But that combination of directions will always lead us back to God.

Find your way back to God.

LOVE RADICALLY

As the blizzard kept dumping snow that night, fear and concern spread among the relatives of 92-year-old Art Huser when he didn't answer their phone calls. So Chris and Cathy Huser, younger relatives of Art, left their home and slowly steered their truck along the treacherous roads until they reached Art's white farmhouse—the place where he has raised and shepherded sheep since his retirement 30 years ago. As the wind howled and the snow stung their faces, Chris and Cathy knocked on the door of Art's home. No answer. Then Chris opened the door with his key. They called for Art and searched through the house, but he wasn't there.

"Do you think he's out in the barn?" Cathy asked Chris, with a combination of fear and hope in her voice.

They trudged through the drifting snow, braced themselves against the driving wind, and opened two gates before they reached the white barn. With the same mixture of hope and fear, they opened the door to the barn. There, they found Art in a scene they will never forget.

"It's snowing to beat the band, it's 10 o'clock at night, and he's out in the barn bottle-feeding his lambs," Chris recalls. "He does whatever it takes for his lambs. They follow him like it says in the Bible—the shepherd and his sheep."

For Art, it was where he was meant to be, reacting in a way that gave meaning to his life. "There are some days when I don't want to get up, but I do because I have to take care of my sheep. I feel good after I take care of my sheep."

Dr. Ellen Einterz knows that feeling of caring so deeply, of giving everything you have. For most of her life, she has befriended people in the African country of Cameroon, providing medical care for endless cases of malaria, malnutrition, cholera and AIDS. It's a commitment that's captured in a story she once shared.

"One Friday night, in the middle of a howling dust storm,

you are trying to start a transfusion on a gasping 7-month-old boy who appears to have not a single vein in his entire body. You are bent over him, ready to try a second or a third stick when suddenly the lights go out. In the darkness, the boy, his eyes rolled back into his head, is struggling for every breath. You could send someone into town to fetch the man who is in charge of the generator, but that would take 45 minutes.

"Or you could leave the ward and go out to the generator house and start the engine yourself, but that would take half an hour, and you don't know whether this child has even 15 minutes of life left in him. So you ask someone to light a kerosene lamp, and by the orange glow you carry on, trying to find the elusive vein in time to keep that life under your hands from going out like the electricity.

"You find it at last, and it is not too late. The blood starts flowing, and not much later, the bony chest starts heaving a little less desperately, and the grey cheeks begin to lose their ghostly pallor, and finally the mother's solemn face relaxes and streams with tears of silent joy. And it occurs to you that that must be one of the most beautiful things it is possible to witness anywhere on earth."

Later, Einterz explains the source of her commitment and her care.

"For me, the bottom line is reading the Gospel and trying to understand how Christ lived and trying to follow it. At every fork in the road, you choose to think about what's right."

✛

Invitation/Challenge: Trying to follow the example of Christ's life is the great desire of all Christians—and the greatest challenge. At nearly every point in his three years of sharing his message, Jesus speaks and acts in ways that show he loves deeply, differently and radically. He not only cares for his sheep, he risks everything in searching for his one lost sheep. In life-and-death situations, he never shies away from the pain, the suffering, the hope and the healing of others; he even experiences all these elements at the same time in his crucifixion.

In their actions, Art Huser and Ellen Einterz sought to live up to the example of Christ's life and his radical love. So did Nathan Trapuzzano, a young man who wrote a touching letter about the way he wanted to live his life and his love, including his desire to be in friendship with God. Nathan wrote the letter after the death of a friend who had died too soon. He wrote the letter to his best friend, Jennifer, the woman who would become his wife in the months ahead.

Nathan's letter was included in a story that I wrote about Jennifer a year after Nathan himself died too soon, at age 24. Here is the letter, the letter that Jennifer also shared with others in her blog entry on the day before the first anniversary of Nathan's death.

Dear Jen,

This morning I found out that an old classmate of mine has died. I was never very close to him, but we did become friends in middle school when we were both into skateboarding and football. As these kinds of things are wont to do, the news made me think of my own life and death. One of my biggest fears is not dying so much as it is leaving my loved ones uncertain, be it about my affections for them, things I may have said to or about them, or even the state of my own soul.

When I die, I want my friends and family—and you especially—to know that I left this world in God's friendship and so await you in heaven for when your own time should come. And as I thought about this, it struck me that the only way to pass on such assurance (to myself not least of all) is to love radically at every moment. For death does not pre-announce itself, not for most people at least. What a terrible thing it would be to die after an argument with you or after sinning against God! To die unreconciled is surely the worst thing that can happen to anyone.

I must continue drinking from the source of love Himself if I am to become a flowing spring to others. Please pray that God will teach me how to love like Him. I love you.

Love, Nate

After sharing Nathan's letter, Jennifer finished her blog entry with a message that was a reminder for everyone else who read it:

"Let us all remember to have faith and love like Nate."

Let us all strive to follow the example of Christ.

Love radically.

SHARE AN INHERITANCE
THAT WILL LAST

As a longtime coach, Bruce Scifres knows the importance of taking advantage of opportunities that can teach his players lessons about sports and life.

As a parent, Scifres also knows the importance of making the most of opportunities that can teach his children lessons about life and love.

Scifres embraced one of those opportunities following a season when his high school football team won another state championship. With that victory, Scifres earned his ninth ring in state championship competition as a coach. When he received the ninth ring, one of his children asked him which of his rings meant the most to him.

Scifres thought about that question for a moment. Then he pulled the nine rings from the boxes where he kept them, and he started to put the rings on his fingers. When he finished, he said to his children, "I'm going to take these off—one by one—until I get to the one that means the most to me. The one that most represents hard work, loyalty, sacrifice and accomplishment."

Continuing the story, Scifres said, "I began to take each of them off and put them back in their boxes—pausing long enough so they could see some of the years and to pique their curiosity. When there was one state ring left on my hand, I quickly covered it with my other hand, took it off and put it in the box before anyone else could see what year it was."

One of his children balked, telling his father he didn't get to see which ring mattered most to him. Scifres told his son, "Yes, you did—because I still have it on." And he raised his left hand, showing his children his wedding band on his ring finger. He told his children, "This is the ring that matters most to me. It represents years of hard work, loyalty, sacrifice and accomplishment. It is, by far, the ring I am most proud of and the one I will never take off."

In sharing that story in an interview and in his book, *Beyond the Goal Line,* Scifres noted, "I wanted them to know that there is nothing in my life that I am prouder of than the fact that I am married to their mother. I believe there is no better way for me to show my love for them."

✛

Invitation/Challenge: Years ago, when my sons were boys just learning the game of basketball, I took them to a youth clinic during a Final Four weekend of the men's NCAA national basketball tournament. I hoped my sons would get a few tips to improve their skills and their knowledge of the game from the college coaches who were chosen to speak to the 1,600 young people. One coach, Peter Roby, shared some advice about life and love that I hoped my sons—and I—would never forget. Here is what Roby said:

"What you have to understand is this: Every day of our life, we wear a uniform. That uniform is the name of your family that you carry with you. It's written across your chest whether you can see it or not. So every day of my life, I try to represent my family the best way I possibly can. I have two children, and the example I try to set for them is that when you have people that love you, you don't do anything to hurt them."

Roby paused for a moment. Then he added, "Tell your mom and dad and those that love you that you love them. Don't wait. When I talk to my mom and dad on the phone, the last thing I say before I hang up is, 'I love you.' Nobody is going to tell me that is not cool. Telling people that care about you that you love them is the coolest thing you can do in your life."

As parents, we strive to instill in our children the faith that guides us, the values that are most important to us, and the qualities that we hope will live in our children's hearts forever. Along with our love, they are the greatest gifts we can give our children.

As our father, God blesses us with an abundance of gifts—our life, our family, our friends, our talents, the hope and promise of each day. Most of all, he offers us the richest inheritance—eternal life with him. He has even given us the two-step guide to receiving this inheritance: Love God, love your neighbor.

What is the inheritance you hope to leave?

Share an inheritance that will last.

GO THE EXTRA MILE

The usual flow of a friendship begins with a connection at school, on a team, in a neighborhood, at work or during a shared interest. If we're blessed, the bond deepens through time, connecting us with someone who not only shares the joy and the fun in life, but also the tough times and the heartbreaking moments.

It was exactly that kind of friendship that Cynthia Kanko needed when she received the devastating news that she had the worst stage of breast cancer. The diagnosis left her reeling: "My world came crashing down. I lost every hope."

Yet there was no one in Kanko's life who she felt she could lean on, or who could help with the pain.

A native of the African country of Ghana, she had moved to Indiana less than two years earlier to pursue a doctoral degree at Indiana University. A single mother, she worried more about her then-10-year-old daughter while she also longed for the comfort of her mom, who was in Ghana. And while she was known, involved and appreciated at St. Paul Catholic Center, she didn't want to burden anyone there. Then one seemingly chance encounter changed everything—not just for Kanko but for a woman she had never met.

That's where the story of the remarkable friendship of Cynthia Kanko and Georgia Frey begins, a friendship that has led both women to believe there are no coincidences with God.

Kanko and Frey first met on a day in July when both women unexpectedly changed their plans. Ever since she had been diagnosed with cancer three months earlier, Kanko hadn't been able to attend Mass at St. Paul Catholic Center because of her weakness from the side effects of chemotherapy. Still, she made a point each week to visit the center's chapel for an hour, realizing "how the presence of the Lord" brought her "a lot of inner peace, joy, comfort and strength."

"Surprisingly enough, in the midst of all this fear, doubt, sorrow, pain and uncertainty about the future—and the countless questions that went through my mind—never once did I question my faith and my God," she recalls. "As unbelievable as it might sound, this rather drew me closer to my God and deepened the little faith that I always had in Christ Jesus."

When she visited the chapel, Kanko usually entered and exited through the back door of the center—"to avoid sympathies from the staff of the parish office." Yet on that July day, she broke from that routine, coming through the main entrance of the church to pick up some reading material. Frey also changed her plans that day.

"I was traveling a lot then, and I was getting ready to go on another trip," recalls Frey, who is also a member of St. Paul's. "I never randomly stop at the church out of the blue. But for some reason, I did."

During her visit, Frey had a conversation with a few other women, including the parish secretary, Valli Youngs. At one point, Youngs mentioned to Frey, "By the way, Cynthia Kanko has cancer." "I said, 'Who is Cynthia?' " Frey recalls. "She said, 'She's the woman who always wears beautiful, traditional African clothes at church.' "

As Frey pictured Kanko in her mind, she also thought of her own diagnosis of breast cancer four years earlier. Even more, she thought of all the fear and uncertainty she felt then, all the radiation and chemotherapy she endured, and all the help she received from others.

"I said, 'Give me her information, and I'll get in touch with her when I get back,' " Frey recalls. As Frey made that promise, Kanko walked in the main entrance of the church and saw Youngs talking with a few other women. Seconds later, Frey and Kanko were introduced to each other. The two women talked for a long time. Then Frey drove Kanko home to her apartment so she would know where Kanko lived.

It was the start of a journey of friendship for the two women, one that neither had expected when they made their fateful visits to church that day.

"I believe the Holy Spirit had a hand in all of that," Frey says.

"Nothing was coincidental that day," Kanko says.

It was just the beginning of the blessings.

When Frey—a wife and a mother—learned she had breast cancer, she turned to the foundations of her life.

"Through my treatment, I had a lot of support from friends, family, the church and the community," she says. "I knew how important it was to get that support. I wanted to make sure Cynthia had a similar support system. I also had some very strong opinions about providers of cancer treatment. Cynthia and I almost basically had the same treatment—chemo first, then surgery, then radiation. So I just gave her advice with the caveat that everybody's experience is different."

Frey has done much more than give advice. She listened to Kanko's concerns and set up a website called Cynthia's Angels. "It's where helpers and volunteers could sign up to help me in various ways," says Kanko. "Some signed up to bring us food, others to go grocery shopping for us, still others to take my daughter to the library and her various programs—all in a bid to help me focus on my healing and recovery without having to stress about minor issues."

In their conversations, Kanko also told Frey about her mother's impact on her life. Knowing how much a mother's support means, Frey tried to find a way to cover the cost of a flight from Ghana, which ranged from $2,500 to $3,000. She contacted a woman she knew from her cancer experience, a businesswoman who decided to donate all of her frequent flier miles to cover the trip to Indiana for Kanko's mom.

"She didn't want any credit for doing it," Frey says.

When insurance didn't cover a substantial part of a medical bill, the members of St. Paul Catholic Center became involved again.

"We got the radiation screening center to hold off on billing her until we could do something as a church," Frey says. "We made appeals in the bulletin and from the pulpit. People were so generous. We got over $10,000."

Frey refers to each of these generous responses as either "another little miracle" or "another God-inspired connection." When she considers all the outpouring of help and prayers that so many people have provided for Kanko, Frey remembers one of the greatest pieces of wisdom that she received during her battle with cancer—wisdom that she believes everyone should embrace during the struggles of their lives. Frey received the advice from Jillian Vandermarks, the director of religious education at St. Paul.

"One of the things I really learned through cancer treatment is that you can say, 'I can do this on my own. I don't want to bother anyone.' When I was sick, Jillian impressed upon me something about all the people who wanted to help. She said, 'All these people are Jesus with skin. Their gift of assistance is a gift from Jesus. These people are put in your life to help you. You have to be open to their help. And accepting their help is a gift for them.' "

Kanko has embraced that gift even as her fight against cancer continues. Her gratitude overflows for all the help she has received, and all the prayers that have been offered for her from Indiana to Ghana.

"My 'angels' give me the strength and the courage to live and fight another day to make cancer a thing of the past," she says. "They all represent Christ here on Earth with dedication and devotion." She becomes especially emotional when she talks about Frey. "Since the day we met, she's been like a sister to me. She's willing to do anything for me. We have a wonderful and beautiful relationship."

All these relationships have strengthened her relationship with God. "My faith remains unchallenged and deepened, and my yoke has been made lighter," she says. "God has been and still is so good to me. I will forever serve him with a joyful heart."

Frey is also there for the long run with Kanko.

"It's been a privilege to witness her courage and

perseverance," Frey says. "The best thing is that 'a forever friendship' has come out of all of this. And it's a reciprocal friendship. It's not just me doing things for her. She's someone I love and trust and like being around, like all my friendships. I just think it was all orchestrated by the big guy—God."

✝

Invitation/Challenge: Only moments remained before the players left the locker room for the game that would decide the championship. Picking up a piece of white chalk, the head coach scrawled on the blackboard, "Win today, and we walk together forever."

Hours later, the players stormed into that locker room again, smiling, shouting, hugging, dancing—knowing they had achieved a moment in time that would bind them all their lives.

Yet to "walk together forever" is not just reserved for championship teams or the world of sports. All meaningful friendships have the quality of "walking together forever." Such friendships frequently begin in the challenging times and transitions of life. In our youth, the uncertainty, fear and intensity of a new beginning in high school and college often leads to bonds that last a lifetime. These friends welcome and support us when we desperately need someone to be there for us. And even if the years, miles and changes weaken that connection to some degree, there's still a fondness for that person, still a sense that in the mind and the heart we "walk together forever." It's the same way with friendships later in life when people reach out to us, support us and stand beside us through the tough times.

Christ gave us the ultimate example of going the extra mile, of "walking together forever," on his path to Calvary. That walk changed everything for us in our relationship with God, fulfilling God's promise of salvation. It's a walk that was also strikingly marked by the fact that Christ didn't make it alone. The night before, none of his friends stood by him, two even betrayed him. Yet as he carried his cross to Calvary, some of the people he loved—and who loved him—were there for him. And a stranger helped carry his cross. That sharing of the cross adds another defining dimension to the connection between God and man—the two walking together toward a moment that would change the world forever. In the same way today, God is there to help us carry our cross.

Go the extra mile in your relationships with God and others, knowing that when you do, you will walk together forever.

Never Limit Yourself—or God

At 90, Lucious Newsom hitches up his blue bib overalls and climbs into his white van, preparing to continue his work as "the Lord's beggar for the poor"—a role he has served for 18 years.

Pulling the van away from the curb, the retired Baptist minister-turned-Catholic waves goodbye to some of the 89 Hispanic families who have just spent the last 30 minutes filling their laundry baskets and milk crates with free tomatoes, onions, peppers and other vegetables—produce that Newsom begged for and collected from a food supply company shortly after he awakened at 4:15 on this sunny, steamy morning.

Now, as a gold crucifix bounces around his neck—a gift from the families he has just helped—Newsom weaves the van toward a place that he views as a beacon of hope and promise in an area scarred by poverty, crime and drugs. The place is called "Anna's House," a clinic and learning center in Indianapolis that offers food, dental care, medical help and educational services, including tutoring and computer training for children. Anna's House is Newsom's dream to make a lasting difference in the lives of people who struggle against the odds. The house is named in honor of Anna Molloy, a 10-year-old blond-haired, brown-eyed girl who helps Newsom feed the poor from her wheelchair.

"I named it for her because of her hard work and her love for Jesus," Newsom says. "She's on oxygen all of the time, and she still keeps coming out to help me."

Newsom parks the van and walks across the street toward Anna's House.

"People have come together," he says, his face beaming. "They said, 'I'll pay for the siding. I'll pay for the plumbing. I'll pay for this and that.' It's more than what I hoped for. It's more than what I dreamed."

The story of Newsom's dream overflows with long hours, complete faith, tireless energy and inspiring anecdotes. Start with the Thanksgiving nearly 20 years ago when he arrived in Indianapolis from Tennessee to serve meals of turkey, potatoes and vegetables for the poor. Newsom loved helping, and he loved seeing the grateful looks on people's faces, so he excitedly asked the other ministers, "What are we going to do tomorrow?" When they told him the event was just once a year, Newsom didn't understand. He wanted to do more. He *had* to do more.

He now helps the poor at several locations across the city. He and his volunteers set up tables and stock them with the fruits, vegetables, salads, breads and meats he has collected—so it looks like a grocery store, so it gives the people a choice and a sense of dignity.

As Newsom stands outside Anna's House, a man from the neighborhood approaches him. The man tells Newsom his electricity has been disconnected and he needs help paying the bill for $149.

"If I get you part of it, how much can you come up with?" Newsom asks.

The man says he needs $60. Newsom gives him the money as the man tells him, "I get upset sometimes, but then I go back and talk to God."

"That's your only hope, man," Newsom says. "I want you to go one time with me to church. I'll take you to Mass."

The man says he'll consider the offer, thanks Newsom again and walks back toward his house. A minute later, a homeless man pushes a shopping cart past Anna's House, a shopping cart that contains crushed cans and a ragged copy of the New Testament. Newsom greets the man like a friend and listens to his story. Newsom promises to return later in the day to help the man get into a shelter. He also gives him $20. The two men hug in the middle of the street.

Two minutes later, a mother walks from her home toward Newsom.

"I've known Lucious for nine years," says the woman, who

is 33. "He's done a lot for this neighborhood. The kids around here don't have nothing but the streets. We haven't had a community center here since I was a teenager."

She then asks Newsom for a favor.

Watching Newsom in these situations, there is a temptation to believe he is "a soft touch." That image is deceiving, says Bill Bahler, a volunteer who has worked with Newsom for eight years.

Bahler shares the story of a man who told him he needed $180 to pay a fine so his wife wouldn't go to jail. After collecting the money from friends, Bahler phoned Newsom to tell him he was giving the money to the man. Newsom told Bahler to hold onto the money for a while, that he would handle the situation. Newsom phoned Bahler back and told him the man confessed that he didn't need the money. When Bahler asked Newsom how he gained that confession from the man, Newsom said, "I told him I was going to represent them before the judge."

"He's taught me discernment," Bahler says. "You don't always give people what they want. You don't always say yes. He expects people to take care of themselves."

Bahler wishes he kept a book of the blessed moments that seem to surround Newsom. One of his favorite stories about Newsom involves a little girl. Newsom befriended the child whose heart was broken when her mother walked out the door of their family's home and never returned, leaving the girl, her sister and their father behind.

"The little girl stopped talking after that, for about three years," Bahler recalls. "Lucious would stop by, talk to her, give her family food and encourage her. One Easter, he took her and her sister to get Easter clothes. As they're leaving the store, the little girl sees a watch and points to it. Lucious asks the sales lady how much it is. She tells him $25. Lucious tells her, ' I spent all my money here, but I want that watch for her.' He told her he would bring the money back, but the lady said she couldn't give it to him.

"He asks to talk to the manager. The manager gave him the

watch and, of course, Lucious later came back and paid for it. After he took the girls home to their father, Lucious was driving away when the father rushed out and stopped him. He wanted him to come inside. 'You've got to hear this,' the father said. When they were inside, the father said to the girl, 'What did you just say?' She said, 'He's a good man.'

"Those were the first words she said in years. Lucious started crying."

That story typifies Newsom, says Bahler. "Lucious tells me, 'Anytime you're doing something spiritual—for someone you don't know and you're not getting anything back either—God is present.' That's what I've learned to expect."

Another friend and volunteer, Pat Fitzgerald, offers this insight about Newsom: "The misnomer here is that he came to Indianapolis to feed the poor. That's not true. The reason he came was to teach us *how to treat the poor*."

To make his point, Fitzgerald shares a story that revolves around an overly ripe cantaloupe that had a few mushy, soft spots. As he held the donated cantaloupe, Fitzgerald remembered his childhood and his saintly mother and how she would have told him that at least one part of that cantaloupe was probably salvageable to eat. So Fitzgerald put the cantaloupe on the table for the poor, which Newsom noticed. He quietly asked Fitzgerald if he would offer rotten fruit to Jesus. When Fitzgerald said no, Newsom softly told him to remove the cantaloupe from the table.

"He said sometime during the day, Jesus would be walking through that line, and we have to offer Jesus the best we have," Fitzgerald recalls. "Lucious said if Jesus came back to earth, these would be the neighborhoods and the people he would come to."

As Anna's House took shape, Pete Molloy learned the power of faith from Newsom.

"I remember sitting down with Lucious and telling him we had to have a major fundraiser to raise $100,000 to build the house," says Molloy, the father of Anna. "He told me I didn't have enough faith. He said what we needed, God will provide. He convinced me to start to reach out, to ask people for what I needed. So many people responded. Lucious' faith has taught me that when you pray and put God in your life, there's no limit to what you can do."

When his cell phone rings, Newsom reaches into a pocket of his bib overalls—the overalls he wears each day "to remind him of what a nobody I am. I try to tell everybody about Jesus because he can meet their needs, he can save them."

The caller wants help with her rent. Newsom offers to pay half, telling the woman she has to help herself. Two minutes later, he's back in the white van, driving to pick up donated clothes that he will distribute to people at a federal housing project in the afternoon. Before his 14-hour day of working for the poor ends, the temperature will reach near his age—90. He keeps going strong.

"I go to bed thankful that God gave me this job," he says. "I'm just thankful I can serve him, that he can use an old guy like me. I live by faith. I'm going to keep doing this until God calls me to heaven."

Invitation/Challenge: It may be the best Gospel story that demonstrates the essential qualities of our most meaningful friendships. The powerful story of Jesus' interaction with the woman who committed adultery certainly provides a revealing insight into the friendship that God offers us.

The story begins when the scribes and Pharisees bring the woman to Jesus, stand her in the middle of them, and then declare, "Teacher, this woman was caught in the very act of committing adultery. Now in the law, Moses commanded us to stone such women. So what do you say?" According to the Gospel of John, which recounts this story, the scribes and Pharisees "said this to test him, so that they could have some charge to bring against him."

Jesus knows their malicious intent. He knows they are trying to use her sin to get to him. Yet instead of attacking their righteousness or worrying about himself, he focuses on saving the woman. He stays calm, coolly bending down and writing on the ground with his finger. He's waiting for the right moment to respond in a way that will let her life be spared.

The Gospel of John continues, "When they continued asking him, he straightened up and said to them, 'Let the one among you who is without sin be the first to throw a stone at her.' Again he bent down and wrote on the ground. And in response, they went away one by one, beginning with the elders. So he was left alone with the woman before him. Then Jesus straightened up and said to her, 'Woman, where are they? Has no one condemned you?' She replied, 'No one, sir.' Then Jesus said, 'Neither do I condemn you. Go, and from now on, do not sin anymore.' "

Let the power of that encounter sink in. It's a moment that connects two people forever, even if they never see each other again. It's also a moment that captures three qualities that mark our best friendships. First, there's the foundation of unconditional support— "I have your back always. I'll go to the wall for you." Second, there's the quality of compassion, looking beyond the person's mistake to still see the value of the person. And third is the quality of accountability—maybe the rarest quality in a friendship, but one that makes it all the more meaningful: encouraging and challenging a friend to strive to reach their potential, their promise.

Once again in this Gospel story, Jesus gives us an example of how to live up to that promise. He doesn't allow himself to be limited by the laws of the past or the threats of the present. He doesn't let the scribes and the Pharisees limit the amount of dignity, care and mercy he will give to another person. And in his compassion for the woman, who was at the edge of death just moments ago, he softly challenges her to not let her sin define her life and her future.

Jesus shows that God always gives his best to us. Lucious Newsom gently instructs his volunteers, "We have to offer Jesus the best we have."

When these two approaches come together, they will form a friendship that has no limits.

Never limit yourself—or God.

LOOK DEEPER

For nearly everyone who goes to a professional baseball game, the great hope is to come home with a souvenir baseball that was used on the field. Having that hope become a reality is even more thrilling when you're 12 and your favorite sport is baseball—a passion that you learned from and share with your father. Which makes the story of what Brendan McCormick did at a game so special. And it becomes even more heartwarming when you learn about Brendan and his dad.

The story begins near the end of a school year when the Indianapolis Indians, a minor league team, hosted an "education outside the classroom" day for schools at their stadium. The idea is to create some educational challenges for students involving the sport of baseball, and then have them enjoy watching a game.

Brendan and the other sixth-grade students at his Catholic school were among the first students in the ballpark, and he and two close friends—Luke Bauer and Johnny Kraege—snagged three front-row seats down the left field line, close to where the Indians' pitchers warmed up in the bullpen area.

As he waited for the game to begin, 12-year-old Brendan noticed a group of third-grade students from another Catholic school settling into seats in a nearby section. He particularly noticed one boy because of the hearing aids and glasses the younger child wore.

Turning his attention back to the field, Brendan watched an Indians' pitcher and catcher warming up before the game when a ball got by the catcher. Hustling to retrieve it, the catcher picked up the ball near where Brendan sat. Then the catcher did something that Brendan never expected. He tossed the ball to Brendan.

As Brendan smiled and held the ball, some of his classmates begged to see and hold the ball while others made offers for him to give it to them. Yet Brendan already had plans for the ball. He immediately moved from his seat and weaved his way through the sections until he was face-to-face with the boy with the hearing aids and the glasses.

He held out the ball to Johnny Malan, a child he was meeting for the first time.

"I said, 'Here you go. Here's the ball,' " Brendan recalls. "He was really happy."

As nice as that moment was, it's only part of the story.

♦

In the section where Johnny sat, one of the school's third-grade teachers had been keeping her eyes on her children. And if there's one thing that's true about third-grade teachers, it's this: They rarely miss anything that happens involving the children in their care. So Kathy Ducote had seen everything that unfolded in that special moment between Brendan and Johnny. And she was moved.

"He did something adults wouldn't do," Ducote recalls. "What he did exhibited what our faith is all about—love your neighbor."

Ducote left her seat and walked toward Brendan and Johnny. On the verge of tears, she thanked Brendan and asked to take a photo of the boys together. After the photo, she asked Brendan his name. When he told her his first name, she took a closer look at his face behind his sunglasses and baseball cap.

"I asked him, 'Are you an Alerding? Oops, a McCormick?' " Ducote recalls.

Brendan said yes to both his mother's maiden name and his family's name. Ducote immediately thought of Laurie and John McCormick, her friends from their high school days together.

Ducote also thought of the devastating reality that, in early February of 2015, John McCormick had been diagnosed with a terminal brain cancer where the average extended life expectancy was another 15 months. And since Brendan had given Johnny the ball in early May of 2016, those 15 months had just about passed.

"I couldn't even fathom watching your dad struggle like that when you're 12," says Ducote, who still struggles at times with the death of her father. "I had my dad more than 40 years, and it's hard for me as an adult."

Her thoughts return to what Brendan did in the midst of that heartbreaking time.

"Okay, it's just a baseball, but that's every kid's dream when they go to a baseball game—to get a ball," Ducote says. "God had an angel in human form that day in Brendan."

◆

No one knows better the relationship between a father and his children than the mother of those children.

Laurie McCormick was attracted to her future husband shortly after he transferred to her high school as a junior when she was a sophomore. John gave a note to Laurie, asking her to give it to one of her fellow cheerleaders for him. She smiled and sweetly told him that he should give the note to *her.* They dated, became high school sweethearts, and married in 1995. Three sons followed: Sean, Kiernan, and Brendan.

As she watched her boys grow through the years, Laurie always marveled at the approach John had as a father. In describing him as "an amazing dad," she offers a list of his guidelines as a parent:

- From the day they are born, make your children your world.
- Teach them to respect others, and to especially look out for people who may need your help.
- Be involved in their lives, asking them questions and talking to them about what matters most to them.
- Show your children to stay close to God by living your faith.
- Always give them your love.

Like his older brothers, Brendan has been blessed by his father's approach to parenting and life. He is also the son who has completely embraced his father's love of baseball.

His closeness with his dad *and* his passion for the sport grew during John's years as a teacher and a baseball coach at three high schools in the Indianapolis area.

"I just really enjoy baseball," Brendan says. "My dad would take me to the games and explain stuff to me. I would sit in the dugout with the players and help out the team."

So a love of baseball and his dad's guidelines to life were ingrained in Brendan on that day in May when the Indians' catcher tossed him the ball.

It was also a time when John was continuing to teach and coach, even as he came home many evenings exhausted.

"When he got the diagnosis, he was determined to fight it and win," Laurie says. "He went back to school, and taught and coached. And he wouldn't miss anything involving our kids. He didn't care how tired he was.

"The first thing he said every day when he got up was, 'Thank you, God, for another day.' He was deeply faithful. He would pray his rosary daily. But he also struggled with why this was happening."

Even if Brendan didn't know his father's struggle of faith, he daily saw the faith and courage his father showed in trying to overcome his physical struggles. And those thoughts and principles of his father were with him as he moved through the crowd that day to give the ball to Johnny Malan.

His father would be the first person that Brendan told about what he did that day.

"When my dad came home, I told him," Brendan says. "He gave me a hug and told me he was proud of me. Then he said, 'I need to lie down.' "

Forty-six days later, Brendan and his brothers Sean and Kiernan spent their last Father's Day with their dad.

By then, John McCormick's courageous effort to make the most of his last 16 months was in its final days. As he rested in hospice, his large, extended Catholic family had gathered to share their memories, their prayers and their love with him one more time. Before the family saw John, Laurie made sure Brendan, Sean and Kiernan had some private time with their dad.

"I gave him a card," Brendan says. "It was very sad. At the time, I'm 12 and I'm about to see my dad die. I wanted to have time with him."

During that time, Brendan thought of one of the last gifts his dad had given him—the extensive collection of baseball cards that John McCormick had collected since he was a boy himself.

"He told me, 'You're the one who loves baseball,'" Brendan says with a smile.

Brendan also smiles when he remembers the last baseball game that he and his father shared together. It was the last game of Brendan's youth baseball league that spring, and John McCormick's friends had arranged for him to see the game from a golf cart. Brendan hit a triple that game, and made a couple of nice plays in the field as his proud father savored the moments.

"My dad insisted on seeing my last game," Brendan says. "I played really good."

John McCormick died four days after that Father's Day—at the age of 44.

At his viewing, more than 1,000 people showed up. Many of them were former students who shared stories of how he made a difference in their lives as a teacher, a coach, a friend and a mentor—including how he bought shoes and food for them in times of need.

All the stories captured the essence of the way her husband lived his life, Laurie says.

"You just give and give, and it becomes who you are," she says.

Then there is the story of what a father taught a son, a story of the moment when a 12-year-boy who loves baseball gives a prized ball to a younger boy.

Brendan still remembers the look on his father's face when he first told him about what he did with the ball.

"I think he felt really good, kind of like, 'I taught my son how to do this. I taught my son to be a good person.'"

✟

Invitation/Challenge: A college professor once gave his students an unusual quiz, consisting of 10 questions. The first nine dealt with course material. But nothing the students had studied prepared them for the 10th question: "Tell me the name of the person who comes into this room and cleans it right after this class ends."

Every student was stumped. Day after day, for most of the semester, the students had seen the cleaning woman enter their room when their class ended. And day after day, the students paid no attention to her. They rushed from the room or talked to the professor and each other.

Some of the students protested the question. All of them thought it was unfair. When the professor collected the quiz, he shared his reasoning for the last question: "If you remember nothing else from this class, remember this: In life, you will meet people from all backgrounds, all levels of income and position. Treat everyone as important. Treat everyone with respect and dignity."

When I learned about that story, it immediately reminded me of a college professor who taught me a valuable lesson after I had made a bone-headed mistake. His nickname was "Black Bart," a professor notorious for his demanding approach to studying the U.S. Constitution and his no-nonsense attitude in the classroom. So it wasn't exactly my smartest move when I walked into his class late one morning and then did something else to disrupt the class.

Black Bart stopped talking and eyed me, a gunslinger sizing up his next victim. I shivered when he finally spoke, telling me to come to his office at an exact time later that day. The bloodshed would be handled neatly, in private, removed from the eyes of classmates who looked at me as a corpse ready to be picked to the bones by vultures.

I'll never forget that meeting. Black Bart started by asking me what career I hoped to enter. When I told him, he talked about writers and reporters he knew. He suggested books to read, experiences to consider. I had given him ammunition to gun me down, and he turned it into an opportunity to educate me, to get to know me better. Just as amazingly, he never mentioned my transgression. Somehow, he knew it wouldn't happen again. His approach to my disrespect is a lesson in generosity that has stayed with me, a lesson in treating someone with respect and dignity that I have tried not to fail again.

One teacher challenges his students to see that every person they meet deserves to be noticed, to be valued. Another teacher sees past the mistake of a student and takes a deeper look at the young person, and his hopes and dreams. In both situations, the teachers don't merely see with their eyes, they see with their hearts.

It's the way that Christ encourages us to live our lives. Often referred to as "Teacher" in the Gospels, Jesus constantly shares lessons and asks questions that challenge us to take a deeper look at our priorities, our beliefs, our choices—*what matters most to us.* He does it all with the intention of guiding us to look *into* our hearts, to see *with* our hearts. He does it all in the hope of leading us to draw closer to God and the people who become part of our lives, whether it's the bond of a lifetime, such as between a parent and a child, or the bond of a moment in time, such as between two children at a baseball game.

Look deeper.

Do Something That Takes
Your Breath Away

M ark Peredo knew he had to do something drastic.
He had just returned from a journey that many people
consider the trip of a lifetime—a journey that often restores a
sense of peace, healing and spirituality to a person's heart and
soul.

Yet after his 27-day, 580-mile walking pilgrimage across the
Camino in France and Spain in late 2016, all that Peredo felt
was a lingering combination of anger and brokenness.

He was still trying to come to terms with the recent death of
his father, who had always been his best friend.

And he was still trying to completely recover emotionally
and physically from the horrific accident in 2015 that nearly
killed him when another driver struck his car head-on at a
high speed—a crash that led Peredo to have eight surgeries and
devastated the dreams that had just come true in his life.

That's when Peredo decided to do something drastic.

He started a search for the driver of the other car, Luke
Hutchins.

"After my return from the Camino, I had a need to seek him
out, to understand, to see if he was okay," Peredo recalls. "There
was still this whole forgiveness I was withholding from Luke. I
was still angry. I knew I needed another way to go. I was trying
to make a forgiveness breakthrough."

During his search for Hutchins, Peredo came across a news
report in which police stated that the accident wasn't the result
of drugs or alcohol, but a medical condition. Hutchins had
an epileptic seizure. For the first time, Peredo realized that
Hutchins had suffered, too, and was likely still suffering.

So when he finally came face to face with Hutchins in the early
part of 2017, Peredo did something that still stuns Hutchins.

"My initial thought was fear," Hutchins recalls about that first meeting which included his father and a brother by his side. "I didn't know whether he was going to start yelling at me."

Instead, Peredo told him he just wanted to meet him, to talk with him. And through conversations with Hutchins and his father, Peredo learned that since the accident Hutchins was unable to work, had become divorced and was still struggling with the effects of epilepsy.

A short time later, Peredo stunned Hutchins again. He shared his plan to help them both heal their brokenness.

Peredo asked Hutchins if he wanted to walk the Camino with him.

"The thought in my mind is that I'm in limbo about the next steps in life," Peredo recalls. "I'm trying to find my purpose, where I fit in. I knew I was still broken. I wasn't whole. I was hoping I could create a way to make something great out of something bad—and he would be a partner with me in this.

"Through nobody's fault, both of us had almost been killed in the accident. I wanted to do this for myself and him—to walk as brothers, to create something positive for our futures."

When Peredo mentioned his plan, Hutchins had never heard of the Camino, where it was, or what it entailed. But the more that Peredo talked, the more Hutchins became swept up in the thought of traveling to a foreign country, of being on an airplane for the first time in his life. Concerns of how the epilepsy might impact him while walking the Camino faded amid the plans of the adventure.

"I had no idea what I was walking into," Hutchins says. "I figured it was the first time I would ever be out of the country, and there was no way I'm going to turn him down."

In the months that followed, Peredo did fundraising for the trip. During that time, he also read "a couple of articles about a couple of people who walked the Camino who had epilepsy," trying to learn more about how the journey might affect Hutchins. Wanting to help protect Hutchins if he fell on the trail, Peredo bought knee pads, elbow pads and a helmet for Hutchins, insisting he wear them when they began walking.

Finally, in late October of 2017, they set out from a small town in France on the ancient pilgrimage path that leads to the shrine of St. James at Santiago de Compostela in northwestern Spain. And on the first day, as the 49-year-old Peredo and the 33-year-old Hutchins walked up a mountain, their journey almost ended in disaster.

"I vomited four times going up the mountain and two times going down the mountain," recalls Hutchins, who was carrying a backpack that weighed about 40 pounds, similar to Peredo's. "I felt Mark took care of me. He took my pack. If he wasn't there, I might have had to stop right there."

Peredo notes, "He's throwing up, and he's throwing up some more. I'm thinking he's going to die. I take his pack. I'm walking up with his backpack and my backpack."

Peredo was also carrying some emotional baggage from the journey he had made on the Camino a year earlier.

In many ways, that 2016 pilgrimage was his attempt to "reset my life" after the accident on April 10, 2015.

That day, the married father of three had been driving to his home in southern Indiana on I-65 South after a meeting in Indianapolis that had secured a deal with a national company for his growing marketing-design business. Shielded by the traffic ahead, he never saw the car, heading northbound, cross the median out of control until it was too late.

"A car was coming at me at 50 to 70 miles an hour," Peredo recalls.

Firefighters used a "jaws of life" device to extract the bloodied Peredo from his smoking, crumpled car. He recalls being put on a stretcher, lifted into an ambulance and rushed to a hospital where the ordeal of six surgeries on a shattered right foot and two surgeries on the shattered right bridge of his face began.

At the same time, Hutchins was rushed by helicopter to a hospital. The accident left his body broken, with fractures of an ankle, a leg, fingers, ribs, a kneecap and a collarbone. His face had to be reconstructed, with a permanent metal plate holding his chin together.

"The police officers were surprised that both of us were even alive," Peredo says.

Yet as horrific as the accident was—an accident that also eventually led him to lose his business—what devastated Peredo even more was the death of his father from cancer on July 28, 2015.

"My dad was my best friend," he says. "When I was a boy, we lived in Bolivia, out in the country. My dad and I would walk in the mountains. As I got older, we came back to the United States. We'd still walk and talk together. Whenever we had issues in our lives, it was always a walk and a talk."

During that first pilgrimage, Peredo often thought of his father as he walked, leading to an emotional moment.

"About the third week in, I finally broke down and cried," he says. "That was after a day when I pushed myself hard. The following morning, I woke up early. I heard my father's voice. It hit me like a brick. I swelled up in tears, and I cried. I felt he was telling me I was doing all right, that he approved."

Peredo also remembered the advice that his father sometimes gave him—to "keep going forward" in life. He followed that advice again as he carried his backpack and Hutchins' backpack on the first day of their Camino journey.

◆

That approach of moving forward also began to work well for Hutchins after that first day.

He stopped smoking within the first few days of the journey, and he began eating lighter meals, relying on more soups and energy drinks that helped with staying hydrated. He and Peredo also stopped by a medical clinic on the Camino where they sought the advice of a doctor about the medicines he was taking for his epilepsy.

"She said if I continued to take all the medicines, I wouldn't be able to continue the walk," Hutchins says. "I was taking eight medicines, and I reduced it down to two."

With all the changes, he felt better, more confident, and on one of the mountains they climbed, he found himself passing other pilgrims. He even stopped to help one of his fellow pilgrims make it up the mountain.

"She gave me a cross from Israel," he recalls.

There was also the night when he danced with some of his fellow pilgrims, the day when a herd of sheep made him smile as they seemed to come out of nowhere, and the stops in the churches, the cathedrals and the small towns along the way—all part of an adventure that he describes as "a brand-new experience into a whole new world."

But there were tough moments, too. He never adjusted to the dormitory-like hostels where they slept with other pilgrims. He struggled when others spoke a language different than English. He missed his two children. And there were times when he feared what would happen if he had a seizure, fell in a ditch and no one found him.

The mostly "ups" and occasional "downs" of the journey for Hutchins seemed to mirror the relationship that he and Peredo had during the pilgrimage. Many times, they opened their souls to each other.

"We talked about each other's families, our life experiences," Hutchins says.

At other times, they became frustrated and irritated with each other. On those days, they walked with other pilgrims, keeping their distance from each other.

"There were moments when you wanted to knock each other's blocks off," Peredo says. "We're human beings. We have our trials and our issues that we deal with. We're not perfect. But what I found on this trip was the peace of walking with him. We became good friends on the trip. My father was my best friend. I consider Luke as closer to a best friend than I've had in years."

Hutchins notes, "I pretty much treat him like my brother."

The depth of their bond overflowed when they sometimes talked about faith. Peredo considers his Catholic faith as an important part of his life, with "a special place in my heart for Mary." Hutchins found his faith growing during the pilgrimage.

"We were talking about faith and his future one day," Peredo recalls. "I was asking him about maybe being a youth pastor. Right then, a rainbow comes out, and church bells are ringing."

Hutchins viewed his frequent sightings of rainbows on the pilgrimage as a sign for him: "It was kind of like a rebirth. I'm a lot stronger in my faith now than I ever was before."

After 40 days and 460 miles of walking, Peredo and Hutchins reached the shrine of St. James at Santiago de Compostela.

By the end of the journey, Hutchins had long ago discarded his helmet, and he suffered only one seizure along the way.

"It was incredible I was able to walk it," he says. "Mark kept encouraging me. When we got to Santiago de Compostela, I was so happy. It was finally mission complete. I can finally go home now. I was missing my kids so bad. It was a really great experience. If I had the chance to do it again, I would."

For Peredo, the second pilgrimage gave him the peace and healing that had eluded him during his first journey along the Camino. He embraced part of that peace and healing with Hutchins in a way he never expected.

"The best parts of walking together for me were being able to joke about stuff," Peredo says. "By the end of the trip, we were talking about the accident and joking about the accident."

He pauses, collecting his thoughts about how far he and Hutchins have come from that moment when their worlds collided.

"For me, going through this process of healing and letting go and not hating is something I needed to do—to prove to myself, to prove to my children that you have to stay the course, and that something good will come from it.

"I wanted to go back because I was broken. Luke wanted to do it because he was broken. We helped each other through this."

⊹

Invitation/Challenge: Their final exams were over, their last term papers finished. The close friends now had a week to share before their college graduation—a week before they would head to different parts of the country, to start different lives without each other. So they vowed to make the most of the time they still had together, filling each day with all the fun and adventures they could imagine. And as the first day slipped past midnight into the early hours of the next day, one of them looked around at the best friends she ever knew and said, "Who's in for staying up to see the sunrise?" So they did. And as the sun peeked above the trees and rose above the lake, they forgot their exhaustion and watched in awe, savoring the beginning of another day of life, another day to be together.

In the hectic pace and the demanding routine of our lives, the ever-present challenge is to never lose sight of the beauty and wonder in the world that God has created, to never lose sight of the special relationships that mark our lives, to never lose sight of the potential for something new and different in us.

Jesus tells us to never take another day for granted—to savor each day instead of thinking that we can keep drawing from an unlimited bank of days. He lived his life with a sense of urgency—*a breathlessness*—to teach, heal and connect with people in the limited time that God gave him. He also found time to slip away from the world, heading into nature to pray and replenish his spirit. In living his life this way, he once again offered us a guide for our lives.

So get up early to see a sunrise. Stay up late to view the brilliance of the stars. Hike through the woods. Stand by the ocean.

Let the beauty and wonder of the world take your breath away. Or get that breathless feeling by challenging yourself to do something you've always wanted to do—take music lessons, write a story, lace up your running or dancing shoes, or make the first stroke on a canvas.

In doing something that leaves us breathless, it opens us to a fresh way of viewing our lives. The senses heighten, the heart beats faster, the adrenaline rushes. And for that moment, life is vivid, intense and breathtaking again.

Yet the true gift comes when we strive to begin each day knowing the beauty and the wonder of the world will be revealed to us in at least some small way—and when we stay open to the opportunities for renewal and discovery in our own lives. And maybe that renewal and discovery comes in our relationships, too. We take a new look and see the gift in a spouse or a friend we have taken for granted. We reach out to someone who has hurt us or someone we have hurt, seeking to find a way to heal the relationship, to heal ourselves.

Maybe we even take a fresh look at our relationship with God. Think again—as if you are learning this news for the first time—that God loves us so much that he sent his son to us, a son who lived in this world and who still wants to live in us. It can leave you breathless.

Do something that takes your breath away.

Live Abundantly

In a moment, Florence "Flo" Spear will explain the touching reason she decided to charge her friends and family $100 each to come to her birthday party.

Right now, though, Flo is talking about the remarkable reaction she had when five doctors surrounded her bed, trying to prepare her for dying.

"They had this funeral look on their faces," Flo recalls. "One of them said, 'We have done all we can do for you, but we are not getting the results we need to keep you alive. You will be comfortable, but don't expect any miracles.' "

Silence filled the room as the doctors expected the natural reaction of tears and despair from Flo. Yet when the 76-year-old woman looked at the doctors, she said, "Here's the deal, guys. Keep me alive for my 77th birthday because seven is a lucky number and, by God, I'm a lucky lady."

That's also when Flo came up with an idea that she considers divinely inspired. She decided to hold a combination birthday party and going-away party for herself—to raise money for an organization that helps women and children who are victims of domestic abuse. It's the kind of grand gesture of generosity and gumption that people have come to expect of her. Her zest for life even shines through in her party invitation that proclaims, "It's the only deal in town where you can get a $2 meal for 100 bucks."

That zest was also there years ago when she approached comedian and former television talk-show host David Letterman with an unusual request. At the time, her grandson was playing baseball in a youth league that needed a new system to water its fields.

"Someone told me Dave had played there," Flo recalls. "I wrote him a stupid letter on a Friday. We got a call from Letterman's attorney on Wednesday, asking how much we needed. The next morning, the money came in the amount of $5,000."

Flo puts her hand over her mouth in horror.

"Oops, I'm not supposed to tell how much money I got. I had to sign a paper. What the hell, I'm dying. They can sue me," she says with a laugh.

The Letterman connection was just beginning. Flo kept telling people how he came up with the money, and how he and his attorney even agreed to sponsor teams in the league. One of her friends then suggested she try to get tickets to his "Late Night" show. Flo did, writing a letter a week for 36 weeks until the tickets came. When Flo and a friend went to New York, a staff member approached her after the show, saying Letterman wanted to meet her. Seeing him, Flo extended her arms and said, "I can't imagine I would get this close to David Letterman and he wouldn't hug me."

Letterman hugged her. She holds up the framed photo of their hug to prove it.

It's vintage Flo. So is the story of her commitment to help women and children who are victims of domestic abuse. She has experienced that abuse. After her husband had died and her two sons had left home, she was beaten by a man she had started dating.

"I got out of that," Flo says. "It lasted one time but long enough to know what it feels like."

When she learned about an organization that provides food, clothing, furniture, housing referrals and job assistance for victims of abuse, she did everything she could to help. And when she received the death notice from her doctors, she instinctively searched for another way to help the organization. She also looked for a way to continue celebrating life, just as she had done 24 years previously when she was diagnosed with cancer.

So she decided to celebrate her 77 years with "a life party," complete with food, drink, music and dancing. And she put up the first $100 at the party, hoping her friends and family would match it or give what they could. Then something wondrous happened. The news of her story, her party and her approach to life spread. More than 300 people attended the party, including many of whom she had never met previously. When the party ended, Flo had raised about $20,000 to help women and children.

To show people how she has always tried to embrace life, Flo included a bookmark in her party invitation. The bookmark has a picture of a single rose in full bloom. It also has her favorite Bible verse: "I came that they may have life, and have it abundantly."

"That's what my life has been based on," Flo says. "I figure if Jesus had that attitude, there must be something to it."

✢

Invitation/Challenge: When I think of my family, I often smile while recalling this quote, "Remember, as far as anyone knows, we're a nice, normal family."

When I think of my brother and my sisters, I find a certain amount of truth in this insight from writer Clara Ortega, "To the outside world, we all grow old. But not to brothers and sisters. We know each other as we always were. We know each other's hearts. We share private family jokes. We remember family feuds and secrets, family griefs and joys. We live outside the touch of time."

When I think of our three children, I have the satisfaction of knowing their bonds run deeper than blood; they are blessed by a closeness that overcomes the distances of their lives.

These thoughts remind me of the blessings that our siblings often add to our lives, offering us that unique connection of family *and* friendship. Still, I was astonished and touched when someone shared a part of a conversation between two sisters, sisters who were both in their 80s and both of deep faith.

The younger woman had come to the hospital where her older sister was in the last days of her life. The older woman looked at her sister and said, "I'll be dying soon." The younger sister responded, "It will be the best day of your life." Her words were greeted with a smile from her older sister, as both women firmly embraced the foundation that has guided their lives—the gift of eternal life with God.

God blesses us with an abundant life, a life that often includes the blessings of brothers and sisters. He also offers us a life that is even richer.

Live abundantly while believing "the best day of your life" is still to come.

Heal A Heart

The fear flashes in their eyes again as the educators recall rushing to the child who was lifeless on the ground.

In one moment, 11-year-old Ethan Velazquez raced across the playground at his school, playing soccer with his friends. In the next moment, he collapsed—becoming immediately unresponsive, showing no signs of breathing.

Stacy Inman-Davidson reached Ethan first, followed soon by Lauren McLaughlin and Lucas Stippler. The three staff members worked quickly to give Ethan CPR, cardio-pulmonary resuscitation.

"I was scared when I ran over to him, seeing him lifeless, not breathing, turning purple," says Inman-Davidson, a recess worker at the time. "I was holding him and talking to him and giving him air. I thought every time I was giving him air, I was giving oxygen to his brain."

McLaughlin joined in, doing chest compressions.

"There was the feeling, 'Oh, my God! Are we doing the right thing?'" says McLaughlin, a kindergarten teacher. "He didn't have a pulse. When we had done one round of 30 compressions, he started to gasp. Then he lost all coloring, he started to foam at the mouth, and there was no pulse again."

As Stippler kept telling Ethan, "Stay with us, Ethan! Stay with us!" the other two continued CPR, trying to revive his heart and keep oxygen flowing into his lungs and brain until the ambulance arrived.

When it did, the paramedics took over Ethan's care, and the emotions suddenly poured from the three educators.

"Stacy had lost a child in a drowning," says Rita Parsons, the school's principal. "When the ambulance came, she just broke down. It's amazing the strength she had."

As the paramedics lifted Ethan into the ambulance, he was still lifeless.

♦

There are certain phone calls that parents never want to get, and the ones that Jenny and Enrique Velazquez received about Ethan that afternoon shook them to their core. Jenny received her phone call first, telling her that Ethan had collapsed on the playground, to come quickly.

"When I see the ambulance and Ethan on the ground and him not responding, never in my mind did I think that his heart had stopped," Jenny recalls.

She rode in the front seat of the ambulance as it rushed her son to the children's hospital. During the frantic ride, she turned to watch the paramedics give Ethan CPR a third time, followed by an attempt to revive his heart with electric shock paddles. It didn't work.

"I told him, 'Ethan, Mommy's here! Please stay with me!' "

The paramedics used the paddles again. This time, his heart started beating.

In the ambulance, Jenny phoned her husband at work, crying as she told Enrique everything that had happened.

"I was scared, but I felt at peace," he recalls. "I told her, 'He will be okay. Talk with God.' "

When their call ended, Enrique had his own talk with God.

"When I talk to God, I know 100 percent he's my father and Ethan's father. I said, 'God, I don't think this is the time for you to take Ethan with you.'

"Then I called Ethan's godfather and my best friends. They're really close to God. I tell them that I need them, that Ethan's had a heart attack.

"When I got into the emergency room, Ethan looks really bad. There were 10 to 15 people in the room—doctors and nurses. When I took Ethan's hand, he's really cold. A lot of his chest is blue. I thought he had passed away."

As a medical team cared for Ethan, his doctors decided to put him in an induced coma.

"The doctor told us that Ethan had a heart attack, and the only thing we can do is wait," Enrique recalls. "He said the next 72 hours are crucial. The doctor said there might be brain damage because he's not sure there was enough oxygen to his brain."

As each day passed, the prayer tree for Ethan grew. Its roots were in the friends and even strangers from the parish and the school community. It also extended to family members in Costa Rico, Guatemala, Mexico and Spain.

"We're close to God," Enrique says. "My faith is strong and big, but this is pain. I don't want this to happen to anyone. I get down on my knees and start praying. I say, 'God, I know you are the best. You are really smart. But give me the opportunity to have Ethan here. Please don't take him yet.' "

One of the people who prayed fervently every day was Inman-Davidson, whose 4-year-old son drowned in a swimming pool at an apartment complex in 2009.

"The whole time Ethan was in the hospital, I felt I had lost my son all over again," says the mother of three daughters. "I was a mess."

Yet three days after Ethan was rushed to the hospital—as his mother prayed the "Our Father" at her son's bedside—all the prayers were answered as Ethan awakened from the coma.

In the days that followed, medical tests were done on Ethan.

"The doctor said, 'Your boy isn't sick. He's 100 percent healthy,' " Enrique says.

"He doesn't have any consequences. The doctor was impressed. He couldn't explain what happened. I said, 'Doctor, it's God.' "

In the months that followed, Ethan celebrated his 12th birthday. His recovery was also celebrated at a school Mass by the community that prayed countless rosaries for him during his time in the hospital. Everyone in the church that day gave Ethan a standing ovation.

"That made me feel really happy," Ethan says. "I was with my friends again. They were glad to see me."

He's back to playing soccer, swimming, playing his guitar and reading the Bible—all the things he used to do. The only difference is that the doctor attached a pacemaker to Ethan's heart—as a precaution.

"Most people who saw me on the playground that day probably didn't think I was going to make it," he says. "God gave me a second chance at life."

He feels the same way about Inman-Davidson, McLaughlin and Stippler.

"They care for me," Ethan says. "They look out for everyone in the school. And they would do anything to save a life."

His parents are ever grateful.

"God stayed with us," his mother says. "God gave me my son again."

"It happened in the right moment in the right place with the right people," says Ethan's father, citing how quickly the school's staff members responded to give his son CPR. "I know that's God. God is love."

The entire experience has also left its mark on the people who initially helped Ethan.

"I hug him every day, and he hugs me back," Inman-Davidson says. "He looks for me. He and I are best friends. Even now, I think about him and worry about him, like he's one of my own kids."

McLaughlin says, "I've told Ethan, 'I wonder what God has planned for you. There's a reason you're still here, kiddo.' "

Stippler, an after-school recess worker who is studying to be a nurse, shakes his head in wonder whenever he sees Ethan.

"People die of this every day," he says. "Everything had to fall into place for him to still be here. After everything that happened and he recovered, he came back to school and gave me a card and a bracelet."

The bracelet is inscribed with this Bible verse from Joshua 1:9, "Be strong and courageous. Do not be terrified; do not be discouraged, for the Lord your God will be with you wherever you go."

Stippler wears the braided bracelet every day as a reminder of the difference that he hopes to make in people's lives as a nurse, as a reminder of the difference everyone made to Ethan, as a reminder of the difference Ethan makes to them.

"I'll never forget his face that day." Stippler says. "He's a miracle walking."

᛭

Invitation/Challenge: They call themselves Road Brothers, the nickname that captures their friendship and the annual journey they make together every autumn. The organizer of the trip calls it a day of "food, football and fellowship" because of the meals, the game and the good times they share. And after a day of traveling in an RV together, laughing together, and eating way too much food together, the eight friends always head home smiling, knowing the day has made their bond tighter.

So when the news spread that one of the Road Brothers had a brother and sister die within a short time, the others came together for their friend. He told them how he was touched by their support. He talked about how hard this time was for him. And soon the conversation took a spiritual turn, with him and several of the other Road Brothers sharing stories of how, as they struggled with the death of a friend or family member, there came times when they felt the presence of that person, or some specific reminder or sign associated with that person—as if they were being assured that the person they loved was fine and perhaps even watching over them.

One of the Road Brothers shared a memory from his childhood, when he and his brother were given chores by their mother to help clean the house, including flipping cushions on the furniture. As an incentive, his mom always hid coins in the couch for her sons. And she later jokingly told him and his brother that even after she died, she would leave coins for them as a sign that she was still with them. Years after her death, during tough times in his life, he has often found coins on the street, making him think of his mother, and making him believe in her continuing presence in his life. Later, he takes the coins to the cemetery where she is buried, and places them at her gravesite.

That story evokes thoughts of the communion of saints that marks our lives of faith—of how we are connected across time, distance and even death with the people we love, the people who love us. The sharing of that story also suggests that for many of us, our healing from the losses that mark our lives is never quite complete. That realization leads me to think of the wisdom that a friend once shared with me. Dr. Chuck Dietzen said that in matters of hope and healing, "God is always present, but he usually makes his presence known in the form of another person."

At some point, we all will reach the edges of life, love and faith. We all will need comfort. We all will need to know that someone cares.

Heal a heart.

Embrace The Gift Of Life

Tony Dungy can delight and inspire audiences with funny and insightful stories from his days as a player and a coach in the National Football League, including his experiences in leading the Indianapolis Colts to a Super Bowl championship. Yet right now, the Pro Football Hall of Fame coach is telling a poignant story from his relationship with his wife, Lauren. The story begins with Dungy recalling a time in their home when the youngest of their three biological children was about nine years old.

"Lauren said, 'Boy, this house is really quiet,' " Dungy recalls. "She wanted to adopt a child. I was OK with it, but really not on board. She did a lot of the legwork first. Then I went in to talk to the person at the agency. When we were finished talking, the lady said, 'Mr. Dungy, you've been awfully quiet. Do you have any questions?'

"I said, 'I have just one. If we decide to do this—I've heard all the horror stories—how long is this going to take?' And she told me something that just pierced me, and made all the difference in the world to me. She said, 'If you're interested in an African-American or biracial child, you could take a child home today.' "

Dungy had believed the process could take as long as a year. After hearing the timetable from the woman, Dungy focused on some of the beliefs that guide his life.

"I thought to myself, 'If I'm saying I'm pro-life and I'm a Christian, and I'm encouraging women to not have abortions and bring these kids to life, I've got to step up and meet that.' "

The Dungys adopted a one-day-old boy. In the years that passed since then, the couple adopted five more children.

"At first, Lauren told me, 'If we could adopt one more child, I think our family would be complete.' And that was number four. And now we've got nine," Dungy says with a laugh. "I should have known it wasn't going to be just one more."

⁜

Invitation/Challenge: I once entered a funeral home to pay my respects to a mother and father whose infant son had died. The child had been born with severe respiratory and neurological problems. He also had other birth defects, all of which led to him spending a significant part of his less-than-one-year life in a children's hospital.

Some people said it was better for the infant and his parents that he died. Surely now, the thought was, the infant will have the peaceful, beautiful life that all children deserve. But when the infant was alive, the parents never gave any indication that it was better for their son to die. Instead, they loved and cared for him. And they swear that he returned their love, and taught them through his pain and suffering.

Standing with the infant's father at the funeral home, I noticed a stuffed animal had been placed in the coffin. I asked the father if it was a favorite toy of his son. He answered, "No, that's a new one that we got for him. We were kind of selfish about his toys. We wanted to keep them for ourselves, to have something of his."

In those words, it was evident that his son had touched his life with love.

That moment also revealed a glimpse of the depth of God's love for us. God knows what it means to have a child die. God knows the pain, the heartbreak, the devastation. Yet he endured it all to offer us the gift of eternal life.

The bond between the father and the infant son mirrors the bond between God the Father and God the Son. Through the pain, the suffering and the death, there are lessons about the power, the purpose and the promise of our lives. Our power is in the love we share in whatever time we have together. Our purpose is to live in such a way that the people whose lives we touch will be blessed by our hope, our joy and our love. Our promise is to be reunited with God, the Father who longs to be with his children.

They're all part of the gift of life we've been given.

Embrace the gift of life.

MAKE THE MOST
OF A SECOND CHANCE

Leo Stenz uses an unusual word as he shares the story of his friendship with Ennis Adams: "Haunting."

In fact, there is not much that is usual about the close bond between Stenz and Adams—especially the way their relationship began.

As the president of a construction company, Stenz has been a longtime, quiet force in the redevelopment of Indianapolis. Beyond buildings, Stenz has also worked to transform the lives of people who live on the streets downtown. He has long helped to coordinate the efforts of a volunteer ministry that provides clothing and a meal for about 200 homeless people every Saturday morning. It was there 15 years ago that Stenz and Adams met. Recalling his life back then, Adams describes it as "a life of drinking, using drugs, being incarcerated, living on the streets, and being close to death." Then he joyfully adds, "God rescued me and helped turn my life around. God came to me through the care and help of another person, my good friend, Leo."

So this is a story of friendship, transformation and faith—a story of two men dealing with their own haunting moments who now work together to help people change their lives.

Just after nine o'clock on a Saturday morning, Stenz and Adams both work the crowd that has lined up in the parking lot of Roberts Park United Methodist Church. It's where the volunteer ministry sets up every week, and it's where the homeless often turn to talk with Stenz and Adams. In Adams, they see a tall, athletic figure who once struggled with the same demons they face on the streets and in their lives. As they talk to him, they seem to want to make sure he's still doing well— viewing his transformation as a sign of hope for them. In Stenz, they see a slim, silver-haired figure with a shy, welcoming smile who asks their names, tries to get them to share their stories, and encourages them to change their lives.

Adams remembers his early days of meeting Stenz.

"Leo always brought a different kind of flavor," Adams recalls. "He brought fun and laughter to whatever he was doing. He brought a little conversation, asking about what was going on with us, what was going on in our families. I looked forward to seeing him. He'd talk to me about stopping drinking and hanging out. His sincerity was always there. I always noticed he had something good to say about the worst ones. The worst of the worst were the ones he navigated to."

Stenz made a point of keeping his focus on Adams during those times.

"Clearly, he was the kingpin of the group," Stenz says. "I saw how the others respected him. I saw they listened to Ennis."

At the time, Stenz didn't know the full details of Adams' life that led him to end up living on the streets. He didn't know that Adams was arrested as a teenager for burglary and spent 5½ years in a juvenile correctional facility. He also didn't know that after Adams' release from prison that Adams married his high school sweetheart and they had three children.

"During this time, I was working, helping take care of the kids, and going to church, but I was living a double life," Adams recalls. "I always found time to hang out on the streets and do drugs on a daily basis. I tried to make it all work together—my job, taking care of the kids, going to church and doing drugs, but something had to give. It eventually caught up to me, and I found myself back in prison and separated from my family.

"When I got out, it was even worse than before. I went right back to the streets. And although I worked a lot, I never had any permanent job. I lived in the streets, drank alcohol and did drugs regularly—and got farther and farther away from my family. This became my way of life, and the years kept going by."

While those choices and decisions haunted Adams, Stenz had his own haunting time in life. Right before Stenz started volunteering, he felt there was something missing in his life. He thought he was too focused on himself.

"I was looking for some way to get out of my own problems of my little world," he recalls. "I have a heart for males who are broken down and don't know how to get back on their feet. I tried to reach out of myself, and it was contagious. When these guys know your name and you know their names, there's a connection. There's a word that St. Ignatius uses to describe that connection—'haunting.' You know them, they know you, and you know they're living down by the river. It keeps you on focus to do everything you can for them."

Part of that effort for Stenz includes offering the men work at his construction sites—sometimes for a day, sometimes for longer.

"I always felt it would be good to get these guys in the routine of a job," he says. "Eighty percent of the time, you're wrong."

It's a success rate that has sometimes led some of Stenz' staff to raise their eyebrows in a look that suggests, "You really want to try this again, boss?"

Stenz keeps trying.

"We give a lot of people a shot. We gave Ennis a shot."

At first, Adams wasn't willing or ready to take advantage of that shot. He had made steps to change his life by entering an alcohol program at the Salvation Army, but his full commitment wasn't there until he came "close to death."

"Leo offered to help me, but I wasn't ready to share with him because I wasn't being honest with myself," Adams recalls. "I wanted to work a program, go to church and continue drinking all at the same time, but it didn't work. I ended up in the hospital, very sick. Finally, I decided that this was it. I got out of the hospital and began working my program with honesty and sincerity. Leo was right there to help me."

Stenz started Adams as a day laborer for his company. And every day, Adams stopped by Stenz's office to thank him for the work and the support.

"Over the years, I saw how Leo kept helping people," Adams says. "They would let him down, and he would still keep helping them. I reached the point where I didn't want to let him down. Then I wanted to get back to my family."

Stenz's willingness to keep giving people chances stems from his embrace of Matthew 18:22, the passage in which Peter asks Jesus how many times he should forgive someone. Christ's answer of "70 times 7" has now become a shared motto between Stenz and Adams.

"Where I felt God was moving me was to encourage people like Ennis. I said, 'Ennis, you have all the right stuff. You have to keep going,' " Stenz says. "I was trying to be a friend. That's how you have to be with these guys. You don't know where God is leading them, but you see they have worth."

Adams has been a permanent, full-time employee of the company for the past seven years. During that time, he has never missed a day of work. He cleans and takes care of the office, the parking structure and the condo area of the company's downtown complex. And every work morning, he is at the entrance of the building, greeting his fellow employees with a smile and words of encouragement.

"It's just going the extra mile," Adams says. "I got that from Leo."

The blessings run both ways.

"There's a bond of friendship," Stenz says. "We have a lot in common. We love sports. We play basketball together. We're able to discuss things. I use him as my street professional. I say, 'What about this guy?' Ennis has taken on a role that says, 'Hey, I've made it, and you can make it, too.' He's following God's prompting."

That prompting has led Adams to be there for the homeless ministry every Saturday morning.

"The guys say, 'We just want to see you,' " Adams says. "I look forward to going down there. Most of the guys just need to be talked to and inspired. I try to encourage them to lead a spiritual life, to reach out to others."

He's also become involved in a retreat program to transform the lives of homeless people.

"I've gotten much closer to God than I've ever been because I spend more time with him. I look forward to telling people where I was and where I am now. By telling my story, I feel as if

God is working through me to help them."

It's a story of renewal.

"I live in my own home. I have a job that I love, and I have many friends," Adams says. "Best of all, I have a great relationship with all three of my children. And for the icing on the cake, all three of them are college graduates. I couldn't be prouder."

It's also the story of two men who have transformed each other's life.

"At this point in our friendship, it's a spiritual friendship," Stenz says. "We can share our faith. We talk about it. That doesn't happen with everybody. We don't hold anything back. He knows my downside, and I know his downside. To me, it's exciting to see someone pull himself up through the grace of God and a lot of perseverance—which Ennis has. And for those who aren't where he is, it's still seeing the face of Christ in them. It encourages me that you can't write the person off. It keeps me balanced and keeps me going."

For Adams, it's all a matter of continuing to strive forward, knowing he has a friend on his side.

"I've learned how to get up after falling down. Part of getting up is helping others so they don't make the same mistakes. I learned that from Leo. And I'm grateful to God for letting me be this way. God has just put this desire in my heart to be a better person."

☩

Invitation/Challenge: Consider this situation: You have a friend who has always wanted the best for you, a friend who has always given you the best of himself. Yet in the toughest moment of his life, a moment when he desperately needs you—if only to know you are there for him—you deny you even know him, letting him fend for himself against people who want to destroy him. And he knows you have done this, and it strikes him to the heart even more than the words and actions of his enemies ever could. Yet when he sees you the next time, he never mentions your shame or your cowardice. Instead, he has already forgiven you in his heart. And he shows his everlasting love for you by asking you to be the lead person—the foundation—for spreading his message to the world. And you embrace that second chance with all your heart and soul.

That's the essence of the friendship between Jesus and St. Peter, the only two people in the history of the world who are known to walk on water—even if it was for the briefest of moments in Peter's case. Yet that truly unique connection isn't what makes their friendship so amazing. At different points in their relationship, Jesus calls Peter "Satan," chastises him for his pride, and publicly declares that Peter will betray him three times in one night. And Peter doubts Jesus even as Jesus stands before him, and he betrays Jesus just as Jesus said he would. Many of us on either side of that kind of friendship would have cut the bond at some point. Yet Jesus keeps seeing the value and the promise of Peter's life, and Peter keeps trying to live up to the potential and the promise that Jesus sees in him. In their actions, we see more than the essence of the friendship between Jesus and Peter. We see the essence of friendship itself. We are also offered a view of the friendship that Jesus extends to all of us—a friendship in which we are given numerous second chances.

It's there for anyone who's ever felt lowly and despised, in the same way that Christ befriended tax collectors, prostitutes and people who were lame. It's also there for anyone who has ever wondered or worried that it's too late to turn to God, as Christ offered that opportunity to the Good Thief dying next to him on the cross.

At some point, we will be called to follow Christ's example—to give a second chance to someone in our lives. And undoubtedly, we will need a second chance in our lives, most likely multiple second chances. God will continue to give us those opportunities for redemption.

Offer someone a second chance. Make the most of a second chance.

PUT YOUR LIFE ON THE LINE
FOR LOVE

One by one, they stood to eulogize the man, recalling his part in one of the great, real-life love stories.

One by one, they remembered his courage and the tremendous risks he took not to betray his love.

Indeed, if there is a moment in life when one's character is revealed forever, Alois Mancl's moment came during the 10th year of his marriage to his wife, Elisabeth.

The year was 1944. They lived in Czechoslovakia then, and the pounding on their door was from German soldiers. The soldiers had come to take Elisabeth, a Jew, to a concentration camp—the same place where her parents, her sister and her sister's small son were killed in gas chambers. The soldiers also came with a choice that challenged Alois to decide which he loved more: his life or his wife.

Here's the choice the Nazis gave Alois: Since you're a Catholic, we will let you go free if you denounce your marriage to your wife. If you don't, you will be assigned to hard labor at the concentration camp.

The couple had already made one heartbreaking decision. They had sent their then-2-year-old son, Vladimir, to hide and live with Alois' relatives for the rest of World War II—not knowing if they would ever see the boy again.

With his own life and the future of their son in danger, Alois still told the soldiers he would go to the concentration camp with his wife. That's how deep his love for her was.

Fortunately, that moment wasn't the last chapter in their love story. Alois and Elisabeth survived the concentration camp because the war ended before the Nazis could kill them. Freed, they reunited with their son. Then they fled Communist-controlled Czechoslovakia, leaving behind their home and possessions. When they arrived in the United States in 1950, they came with $50, joining other relatives who lived in America.

For years, Alois worked as a musician while Elisabeth worked in an office. In their last years, they lived in a nursing home where they roomed together and held hands as they walked the halls. Alois also sometimes played the piano for her.

Their closeness even continued in death. After Elisabeth died, Alois followed her seven months later. He passed away three minutes after he finished a phone conversation with his only child.

"I guess for him, that was his goodbye to me," Vladimir said after the funeral. "They said his heart just stopped. I don't think he had the spirit to go on.

"You hear about that with older couples, that when one goes, the other goes shortly after. Even though my mother wasn't active or responsive in the last two years of her life, he was there for her. He was determined to take care of her. And when she died, he wanted to be with her."

Their son looked back on his parents' life and love together. He recalled the choices that his father made in life-and-death moments. He remembered the great love his father showed in a time of heartbreaking inhumanity. And he took solace in knowing his parents were together again.

"My mother and I were his focus," Vladimir said. "He taught me that sometimes you have to stand up for yourself even though it might mean you'll be harmed."

Invitation/Challenge: One choice can define a life. Pilate washes his hands. Judas takes the blood money. Mary says "yes" to being the mother of Jesus. Alois Mancl says "no" to denouncing his marriage to his wife.

In life-and-death situations, Pilate and Judas let fear guide them. Mary and Alois let love guide them.

Considering the extraordinary circumstances of their

situations, including their times in history, both Mary and Alois make choices that evoke the highest levels of awe, admiration and inspiration. At the same time, their choices, when stripped to their essence, are also life-affirming because of how blessedly ordinary they are. A woman consents to give birth to a child. A husband upholds his vows to stay true to his wife.

Every day in our lives, the choice of love continues to unfold in extraordinarily ordinary ways. It's there when someone drops to a knee to ask someone to share a lifetime. It's there when a couple welcomes a child into their life. It's there when a parent nurses a sick child through the night or when a grown child stays by the bed of a parent in the hospital. It's there when an elderly person serves as the caretaker for a spouse who suffers from Alzheimer's, a spouse who no longer remembers the life and the love they've shared. In each situation, the fullness of Mary's "yes" shines through, as does the total commitment of Alois. And each choice defines a life.

What is the situation in your life where God is asking you to make a choice that defines you?

Put your life on the line for love.

Commit to Being Great—for Others

As a motivational speaker, legendary football coach Lou Holtz often relies on humor to win over an audience. Consider his comment about how to be happy: "Happiness is nothing more than having a poor memory. If you can't remember what happened yesterday, you feel pretty good today."

He even directs his humor at himself, including this memory from his days as the football coach at the University of Arkansas: "After one big victory when I was at Arkansas, I was put in the Arkansas Hall of Fame and a stamp was issued with my name on it. But the next year, we lost to Texas, and they had to take me off the stamp. People were spitting on the wrong side."

He also jokes about questioning his Catholic faith as a boy: "In seventh grade, I had a nun named Sister Mary Harriet who disliked me and probably with good justification. Because there are certain things about Catholicism that I really didn't like. For example, I don't like fish, and there was a time year-round when Catholics couldn't eat meat on Friday. So every Friday, I'd complain to her, 'I wish the Apostles had been ranchers rather than fishermen.' And I always asked her the questions she couldn't answer: 'Why did Paul keep writing to the Corinthians when they never wrote him back?' "

While leaving his audiences smiling and laughing, Holtz also laces his talks with serious stories, insights and questions about life. One of his most poignant stories concerns his wife of more than 50 years, Beth, who has recovered from cancer.

"My wife doesn't do many interviews because she said one person in the public life is enough," Holtz says. "But she gave one interview … and that was about her cancer. I'll never forget, the question was, 'What did you learn from having cancer?' She said, 'I learned how much my family loved me.' "
Pausing, Holtz adds, "We didn't love her anymore because she

had cancer. We *showed* her more. Isn't it a shame that we have to let somebody have a catastrophe before we say, 'We love you. We appreciate how special you are.' "

Holtz also shares the story of how his wife's advice about avoiding bitterness eventually led to helping him gain his dream job as the head football coach at the University of Notre Dame.

"There's not an individual in this room who doesn't have a right to be bitter," Holtz tells his audience. "At the University of Arkansas, we were there for seven years—seven bowl bids, four top 10 finishes, ran an honest program, graduated our athletes. Yet after seven years, on a Sunday morning, I got fired. They would not give me a reason. I was so mad. I wanted to go to the media. I wanted to blast everybody. My wife said, 'No, you know what we'll do? We'll move on. We're not going to be bitter.'

"We went to (the University of) Minnesota. Two years later, Notre Dame is looking for a football coach. They called Frank Broyles, the guy that fired me. They said, 'What about Coach Holtz?' He said, 'If you can, hire him immediately. The dumbest thing I ever did was let him go.'

"I ended up at Notre Dame because of the guy who fired me at Arkansas. And the only thing that saved me was my wife not allowing me to be bitter."

Holtz encourages the same approach to life that he always had for his players: Keep striving to improve.

"There's a rule of life that says you're either growing or you're dying. Trees either grow or they're dying. So does grass. So does a marriage. So does a business. So does a person. It doesn't have anything to do with age. It has everything to do with, 'Are you trying to maintain or are you trying to get better?'

"Any time you're trying to maintain in this world, you never have a reason to celebrate, you never have new ideas. Being enthusiastic about what you do is critical. It's about having dreams and goals. Regardless of what age you are, there have to be things you want to accomplish, things you want to do."

For Holtz, life essentially comes down to tackling two sets of questions. It starts with the one set of questions that Holtz believes we all need to ask ourselves.

"If I didn't show up, who would miss me and why? If you didn't go home, would your family miss you? And if they did, why? If you didn't show up for work on Monday, would anybody miss you? We should all aspire to make sure that we live our lives in such a way that if we didn't show up, somebody would miss us. Not because we're valuable. Not because we're talented. But because we add value to other people's lives."

The second set of questions to be considered includes the three that everyone will ask about us, Holtz believes.

"Everybody has three questions," Holtz says. "I don't care if you're in business, married or a football coach. Number one, 'Can I trust you?' Without trust, there can be no relationship, and the only way you can have trust is when both sides do the right thing.

"The second question is, 'Are you committed to excellence?' That can only be answered if you do everything to the very best of your ability.

"And the last question everybody asks is, 'Do you care about me?' That can only be done when you reach out and show people on a consistent basis that you care.

"I guarantee you, the person you admire and respect, you've said 'yes' to all three questions."

Invitation/Challenge: A few years ago, I came across a Bible verse that has stayed with me and challenged me ever since. It's from the Gospel of John, "He must increase; I must decrease" (John 3:30). Obviously, the words are a call to make Christ the greater focus in our lives while lessening our obsession with ourselves. At the same time, the more I've thought about these words, the more I've realized that they also could—and should—apply to other relationships in my life: as a spouse, as a parent, as a son, as a sibling, as a friend. I must decrease in my focus on my desires, my wants and my needs while increasing my awareness of the other person's desires, wants and needs.

Imagine the potential of a marriage, a friendship, a

parent-child relationship when both parties follow the approach of "I must decrease, you must increase." It would be amazing. Of course, it's also amazingly hard for many of us to do—to put the needs and desires of someone else ahead of our own. At least it's a struggle for me. Yet in the times I've been successful in those efforts, I've moved closer to that person. It also has moved me closer to God. So, in decreasing our emphasis on ourselves, we increase the potential to deepen our relationships *and* become a better, more valued individual.

Embrace those six words—"I must decrease, you must increase"—and you'll always have the right answer to Holtz' question, "Are you trying to maintain or are you trying to get better?" Embrace those six words in your relationships and you'll surpass the standard of Holtz' challenge: "We should all aspire to make sure that we live our lives in such a way that if we didn't show up, somebody would miss us. Not because we're valuable. Not because we're talented. But because we add value to other people's lives."

Commit to being great—for others.

LIVE YOUR DREAM, AND MAKE SOMEONE ELSE'S COME TRUE

Marc Konesco keeps pushing himself to live outside his comfort zone, believing that's "where the magic happens" in life.

Yet as he and his wife Jen and their three children—all under 10 at the time—were in the midst of their 17-month ocean journey by boat, Marc experienced a moment that made him feel *too uncomfortable*.

"We were at a remote island—a two-day trip from civilization," Marc recalls. "I couldn't start the engine, and our water-maker on the boat stopped working. So here we are, in a remote place, with no engine and no water. I said a prayer, 'Lord, I'm hurting.' Then I ended up getting on the radio, asking for help. The radio could reach up to 60 miles, but I didn't think anyone was around. I was very anxious."

Less than five minutes later, a small boat with two men aboard appeared around a curve of the island, heading toward the family's boat.

"They were brothers," Marc says. "The one brother installed water makers for a living, and the second brother owned a shop where they worked on engines. They were like two angels that came out of the air. After about four hours of working on the boat, we were ready to go."

He pauses before adding, "It shows you how God works."

Sharing that story makes Marc smile. It also takes him back to the time he wrote 15 goals for the "adventure-service journey" that would eventually lead his family to a stronger faith, a deeper connection with each other, and a commitment to serve at an orphanage in Costa Rica for six months.

The first goal on that list notes: "To have the Lord lead us and focus on his will for the rest of our life, fully trusting that his hand is leading this journey."

The Konesco family made their journey from January 2014 to May 2015, sailing the Atlantic Ocean south from Florida and all around the Bahamas. Yet the dream of this trip began even before Jen and Marc were married in 1999. During their engagement, the couple wrote down their dream of someday leaving their jobs and spending a couple of years on an "adventure-service journey." Fourteen years later—in 2013— they steered their dream toward reality when they bought a boat they named *Adagio*.

"It's a musical term to slow the tempo down," Marc explains. "We wanted to slow our lifestyle down."

It was just the beginning of the adventure.

They put their home up for sale in July of 2013 and sold it nine days later. They gave away or sold 80 percent of their possessions. Jen and Marc also took turns getting weeks of extensive training in sailing on the ocean while they alternated taking care of their children. And when the family moved to Florida in January of 2014, they spent several weeks in port, doing practice sails, working on safety drills, and getting used to living together in much smaller quarters—making the transition from their 4,000-square-foot home to their 350-square-foot boat.

In late February of 2014, they left the safe harbor of their lives and set sail toward the Bahamas with their three children— then-8-year-old Joellen, 6-year-old Camden and 2-year-old Maria. Aboard the ship were four months of provisions, including diapers, batteries, pasta and canned goods. Jen had also packed all the materials she needed to homeschool the children. Still, Marc and Jen were hoping to give their children an education that extended far beyond school lessons.

One of the 15 goals for the journey was "to appreciate nature and particularly the ocean to the fullest." That goal was met quickly as the family sailed into the Bahamas in March, a month when they normally experienced the tail end of another brutal Midwestern winter. Instead, they soaked in the sunshine, the blue skies and the crystal clear, turquoise water. And when they docked at a marina in Bimini and were greeted by a dock master who said, "Ya, mon, take any spot you want," they took the first step toward achieving another goal—"to meet a variety of different people."

Before long, they met a woman from France—a paraplegic—who was sailing through the Bahamas with a friend. After Mass one day, they befriended the priest who celebrated it—a priest from Poland who was marking the 50th anniversary of his ordination.

They also met the unusual crew of a boat named *Beacon Won*.

"It was full of high school kids, parents and the crew," wrote Jen in the family's blog, "Love at First Sail," about the group that was volunteering during spring break at an HIV/AIDS camp in the Bahamas. "They invited our family to join them. The plan was to just spend time with the residents, praying and singing with them. Here in the Bahamas, there is still the stigma with those with AIDS, and many families turn their backs on a family member that has AIDS. A former leper colony has been transformed into a HIV/AIDS camp run by a couple from the U.S. It just so happened there were five extra seats in one of the vans. God always works it out, doesn't he?"

The next day, they met the camp's residents, some of whom were bedridden while others were in wheelchairs. The family joined the volunteer group in singing with the residents and listening to their stories. The experience led Jen to write, "It was a reminder from God that no matter where you go, even in the midst of paradise, there are people who need help and need to know there are people who care."

That belief also guided the family as they beached their sailboat for six months to volunteer at an orphanage in Costa Rica. The Konescos moved to that mountainous Central American country during the hurricane season—from July through December of 2014.

"We weren't sure how the Lord would use us at the orphanage," Marc says. "We went to the orphanage five days a week. We cleaned, cooked and organized. We taught English, we taught science, and we played. We tried to follow the best advice someone gave us, 'Don't go to try to do something. Just go to share God's love.' "

The family did that and more, according to Cherie McCullah, the director of the Residencia de Vida orphanage. Marc used his extensive business background to help with the orphanage's financial concerns. He also coordinated the effort to move the orphanage from one site to a new one.

"They came over and fixed meals for us on my days to cook and made it a fun activity for the kids," McCullah says. "They had swimming parties for us. They bought vegetables for us at the farmers' market. The kids loved when their whole family came over because it was going to be a fun time."

She recalls one joy-filled moment that involved a water fight between Marc and the children at the orphanage.

"The kids got squirt guns for Christmas and couldn't wait for Marc to come over that day so they could get him wet. I warned him beforehand so he could have some extra clothes. When he drove up, the water fight started and everyone had a blast. He actually snuck up and got a couple of guns the kids had laying there, waiting for him to come. He got a few of them wet first. The kids laughed and laughed about Marc getting them first."

While the Konescos left a lasting impact on McCullah and the children at the orphanage, the 17-month journey also left its marks on Jen, Marc and their children. Joellen grew in "the depth and understanding of her faith in a pretty remarkable way," says her father. Camden developed a passion for fishing that led to him hooking a 65-pounder that he decided to share as the main part of a meal with other fishers and their families. And Maria developed an early understanding of Spanish, learning the language as the family volunteered at the orphanage.

As their journey neared its end, Jen used the family's blog to share one of the main lessons she has learned: "We have realized that we don't need as much as we used to think we did. Living on a boat forces you to live with less."

She also offered a thank you.

"God has blessed us through this journey, and we thank

him for keeping us safe and somewhat sane—living on a boat can drive you truly insane at times. Every night before we fall asleep, Marc and I pray together. We pray for safe travels and health. We also thank God every night for allowing us to experience this beautiful world he has created."

Marc sees the impact that following their dream has had on his family.

"It's brought a close family even closer, and it's showed our kids and Jen and me the power of dreams and prayers."

The journey also led them closer to God.

"Looking back, I see God's hand leading us to the people, places and events he wanted us to experience," Marc says. "He allowed the Holy Spirit to guide us. We've experienced God's power and grace so many times. After this trip, we are a lot more free and confident in trusting God's guidance for where we are going."

✛

Invitation/Challenge: Jameer Nelson has had a long and successful career as a player in the National Basketball Association. He's even been an NBA All-Star. Yet perhaps his most defining moment in sports came off the court, when he played for St. Joseph's College in Philadelphia. It happened before the beginning of a season when Nelson would become the national college player of the year. During pre-season practices, a few non-scholarship players tried out for the team. One of the players—Andrew Koefer—caught Nelson's attention and admiration because of his hard work, hustle and unselfishness. Still, head coach Phil Martelli was planning to cut Koefer until Nelson interceded, telling his coach that he was just the kind of player who could help their team. Martelli listened to Nelson's plea and kept Koefer on the team. Later, Nelson explained why he made the extra effort for Koefer: "A lot of dreams don't come true in life. If you can make someone's dream come true, you should."

Most dreams begin with a stirring in a person's heart and

soul that can't be ignored, that must be embraced. So in the journey of pursuing a dream, there's a tendency to believe that all a person needs to make it come true is a laser-like focus and a complete commitment of faith and energy. One person alone can will a dream to life—or so the myth suggests. Yet that myth rarely holds true when the journey of a dream fulfilled is examined. At different turning points and potential roadblocks, other people help and guide the dreamer—often unexpectedly. And the journey also sometimes leads to situations where the dreamer helps and guides others. Then there are the moments that can only be explained by God's grace.

All those elements were part of God's greatest plan, his greatest dream—the journey of Jesus on Earth. If there's one quality that most people attribute to God, it's his ability to will whatever he wants to happen. Instead, he sent his son into the world, touching his life with the usual foundation of family and friends, and the unlikely connection with prostitutes and tax collectors. In the last part of his journey, Christ desires to heal people as much as they need his healing. And beyond his time for prayer, he rarely pursued his life's work—God's plan of salvation for humanity—alone. He still doesn't. He still wants people by his side, helping him spread his message.

What is your dream?

Whatever it is, know that other people will help and guide you. Know that you will have opportunities to help and guide others. Know that God's grace will be with you.

Live your dream, and make someone else's come true.

Change the Color
of Your World

It all has to do with the incredible depth of a mother's love. There's no other way to explain what Tina Settles has created, what she believes in, and what she holds close to her heart.

For two years, Settles worked tirelessly to turn an overgrown patch of land behind a church into a flowing garden of red, yellow, pink and purple flowers that has become a home to a dazzling, breathtaking assortment of butterflies. Yet even more dramatically, that change in landscape has led to a special place that has lightly touched upon the hearts and souls of people who have known the unbearable heartbreak of losing a child.

It's a devastation that Settles has suffered personally, too.

This then is a story of transformation, the transformation of a parent—from a mother who never felt so alone and devastated after the death of her only child to a woman who has created a Children's Memorial Butterfly Garden where people can feel some measure of hope and healing as they remember a child who died too soon, who touched their lives forever.

Settles knows that some of the pain from the death of her son, Jeremiah Allen Monroe, will always be with her. And while she prefers to keep private the details surrounding his death at age 29, she openly shares the heartbreak of losing her only child—and the startling discovery she made in the midst of that heartache.

"When I lost my son, I felt very alone," she recalls. "A lot of people at the showing would tell me they had lost a child. I had no clue. Here I was feeling all alone, and other people had been through it. If you outlive your child, it's a strange feeling. I saw they were going on with their lives, and it gave me hope that I would learn, too. I'm still in the learning process."

One significant part that has helped in that process has

happened at the church where Settles and her husband, Kevin, are members. A flower garden behind the church had become overgrown, and there was a plan to return it to grass. Hearing about the plan, Settles asked if she could take over care of the garden. One of the main reasons she wanted to do it was because she remembered how much her son enjoyed watching her garden.

"I thought it would be a good diversion for me," she says. "I was so depressed. For me, gardening is therapeutic. Some of the flowers that were originally there, once the weeds were pulled away, we started to see butterflies. Then I added some flowers and weeds that attract butterflies. We have wild violets. We have milkweed. If you don't have milkweed, you won't have monarch butterflies."

The butterflies appealed to Settles' sense of beauty, but there was another reason she strived to make them so essential to the garden.

"When you think of butterflies, they're like our children. You think of their metamorphosis—from a caterpillar to a butterfly. It's kind of like the Resurrection. As the Bible tells us, when we pass, we turn into something beautiful. It's a reminder that our children will be resurrected, and their spirits are safe with God."

As the garden began to take shape, so did her idea of wanting to have a plaque in the garden that remembered her son and the children that other parents had lost.

"I started thinking about all the people who had been there for me, and the stories they told me about losing their children. We remember our children in our hearts always, but I thought it would be nice for our church to remember our children, too. The children on the plaque are of all ages. One person lost a child at 56. That was still her child."

Years have passed since her son died, but there are still times that test her soul.

"There have been people who told me that some people never get over losing a child. For me, it's very hard. He's the only child I've ever had. But I believe he's with God. He no longer suffers or knows pain. And I believe I'm starting to heal. But you just never want to forget them. When I'm at the garden, I think of him. When I feel sad, I can sit on the bench and feel God's presence."

She walks through the garden, taking time to kneel and weed. She also looks for the butterflies—the monarchs, the black swallow tails, the tiger swallow tails. They grace the garden on most days, especially in the morning or after a rain. She smiles and points to a butterfly alighting on a purple flower.

"I wanted to turn something sad in my life into something good. I wouldn't be where I am right now if it wasn't for my faith. When you're down and people are there for you, that's when you see Christ's face."

☩

Invitation/Challenge: The most dramatic changes in our lives are always personal. The life-changing moments can begin in childhood with a family's move to another city or the divorce of parents. The transitions can continue when a young adult leaves behind family and friends to attend college or start a career in a different part of the country. There are also the changes that come with marriage, the arrival of children, and the beginning months for a married couple when the last child has left home. Many of these life changes involve moments of saying goodbye, and promises of staying in touch. Then there are the moments of final goodbyes when a family member or a friend dies.

Uplifted by Christ's resurrection, our faith leads us to believe that every goodbye—including a final goodbye—is another beginning, another opportunity for transformation. Even in our suffering, we can be transformed, deepening our compassion and connection with others who experience pain and loss. In that transformation, we become more aware of the gift that life is—and the people who touch our lives. And when this life ends, there is the hope of life with God. The beauty and wonder of this transformation are poetically captured in the English proverb, "Just when the caterpillar thought the world was over, it became a butterfly."

Still, the hope-filled marvel of the butterfly isn't complete without another essential quality: courage. It's the down-to-earth courage needed for such a transformation to take flight—the daily courage a person summons to live through pain and loss. Hope leads to courage, and courage leads to hope. That connection is expressed by a woman who created a vibrant touch of beauty and solace for herself—and others—from the darkest moment of her life: "I wanted to turn something sad in my life into something good."

Change the color of your world.

MAKE GOD CHEER

This story is about teenagers—their strength, their dreams, their vulnerability and their desire to belong to and contribute to something bigger than themselves.

It's also a story about parents—how they love their children, worry about them, bleed for them, cheer for them and hope they will learn their worth in the world.

This story is also about friends and teammates—how they look out for each other, extend their hands and their hearts to each other, and how, as they come together to pursue wins and championships, they sometimes grasp a greater success: becoming part of a group that not only strives to reach its potential as athletes who dare to dream, but also as people who dare to care, especially about one another.

It's a story that could take place in any high school across the country, and in any sport being played. Yet this story begins on a football field on a Friday night beneath the glow of a stadium's lights. The game has ended, and the football players and coaches of Bishop Chatard High School start to join together on the field, where they will eventually kneel in the grass and the dirt together to offer a prayer of thanks for having had the opportunity to play and compete.

From the Bishop Chatard sideline, Will Kuhn directs his motorized scooter toward that area of the field, his eyes looking up at the backs of several of his teammates who tower above him and walk ahead of him in their uniforms and helmets.

Will is a member of the team as a manager, a youth who has a passion for football and a nearly lifelong dream of wanting to play the game. But he was diagnosed in kindergarten with Duchenne's muscular dystrophy, a degenerative and progressive form of the disease that causes people to lose the use of their muscles—starting in the legs, then the arms, then the lungs and the heart. It's a form of muscular dystrophy that also comes with a shortened life expectancy.

As a boy, Will could walk and even run. By 13, those movements were no longer possible. At this point in his life, the disease has robbed him of the physical ability to do basic things that most people take for granted.

"He can't walk, he can't brush his teeth, he can't comb his hair, he can't get out of bed by himself," says his mother, Kathy Kuhn. "Yet it doesn't really keep him from doing the things he wants to do, the things that normal seniors in high school do."

As Will steers his scooter toward the middle of the field, Kathy Kuhn watches him with her usual motherly mixture of great pride and constant concern. She has been cheering for the oldest of her four children all his life, drawing strength from the way he keeps moving forward against incredible odds. Her nickname for Will is "Superman" because, she explains, he is the strongest person she has ever met.

She also knows his deepest desires, which include a desire that nearly every teenager has—to be included as part of a group. For Will, that desire has always been a measuring stick for feeling "normal," a feeling that has been a reality for him ever since he became a part of the Bishop Chatard football program.

Kathy Kuhn still remembers the phone call that she received from Bishop Chatard's head freshman football coach, Rob Doyle, during the summer before Will entered high school. Doyle had heard that Will had been a manager for the football team at his grade school, and wanted to know if he would like to help with the freshman team. Three years later, that invitation from Doyle still means so much to Will's mom.

So does the conversation that she had with the school's varsity head coach, Vince Lorenzano, during the second football game of Will's sophomore year—when Will first became a manager for the varsity team.

At halftime, Lorenzano walked by the stands where Kathy Kuhn was sitting, wanting to talk to her about Will. As Kathy recalls it, Lorenzano yelled to her, "Hey, Kuhn, he doesn't want to go to the football game with his mommy."

"I had taken William to the game because he needed his scooter to get around," Kathy recalls. "So I said to Coach Lorenzano, 'Well, Coach, he can't walk. How else is he going to get here?' And Coach said, 'We're football players. We'll get him and the scooter on the bus.'

"The following Friday, Ricky Rivelli piggy-backed William onto the bus, two or three boys lifted his scooter and put it into the luggage compartment with all the football equipment, and they went off. For William, he was part of the team.

"A couple of weeks after that, I went up to Coach and said, 'Thank you so much. You can't imagine what this is doing for William.' And Coach looked at me and said, 'It's not about what we are doing for him. It's what he does for us.'

"I walked away crying."

Lorenzano doesn't mention those stories when he is asked about any moments that stand out from Will being part of the football program. Instead, he talks about Will often leading the stretching part of practice for the players by blowing a whistle to start each drill. He also mentions Will being out on the field through the heat, rain, mud, cold and snow—elements that are all part of a football season.

"He's one of those guys who doesn't let anything stop him from living life," Lorenzano says. "His attitude is the key. No matter how he feels, he's out there. Part of what we stress as a program is to stay even-keel. We don't live in a perfect world. We don't have perfect bodies. But we deal with it. Will deals with it. He does everything we do. For guys who take the time to understand the situation—and I think our players do—they appreciate what they have. I know those kids love him and would do anything for him."

Count Mike Goetz as a loyal member of the Will Kuhn fan club. A fellow senior and a football player, Mike has a quiet, respectful attitude toward adults and a tough, give-everything-you-have approach to playing football. He is the one who now piggy-backs Will on and off the bus on game nights.

"We've been friends since freshman year," Mike says. "I really didn't know what to expect at first. Meeting Will and seeing what he's about has been a great experience for us. He's just a normal kid to us. From Will, I've learned that when you're put in a rough situation, you have to make the best of it. It's all about brotherhood and looking out for each other. When we go on the field together, it's like a magical bond."

It's the magic that teams and teenagers can know when they reach beyond themselves and when they reach out to each other. It's the magic that glows on Will's face and in his eyes when he talks about being part of one of those teams.

"Football has been a passion for me for many years," says Will, whose father, Walt Kuhn, is also a major influence in his life. "When I was growing up, I really wanted to play football. I wish I could play. I just enjoy the way you work together as a team.

"When I came to Chatard, it was a real life-changing experience. The seniors don't just hang out with the seniors. We hang out with the underclassmen, too. I know I'm in good hands with the football team. They are my extra helpers at school. It makes my parents feel good. It makes me feel good."

One of his favorite moments from his senior season so far occurred when the 26 seniors on the team spent time together at a lake house for a pre-season bonding experience. For Will, it was an opportunity to get to know his teammates away from the sport that unites them.

"It was really cool. I got to find out a little more what people were thinking about," Will says.

The scene shifts from friends talking around a fire back to the football field on that Friday night under the glowing lights when Will leads his motorized scooter from the sidelines toward the area where the players and coaches are getting ready to say a post-game prayer of thanks. On the way there, Will's scooter gets stuck in a rut on the field—a common occurrence during the season when the combination of rain, mud and cleats can create grooves and dips on a field.

Watching from the stands, Kathy Kuhn used to worry about

Will in such moments. But the history of four high school football seasons has taught her to leave behind those worries.

A moment later, one of Will's teammates moves behind his scooter and pushes it forward, out of the rut. He continues pushing Will to where the rest of the team kneels in the grass and the dirt. Neither Will nor his teammate give any indication that what just happened is anything special. They both share this belief: It's what teammates who have experienced and endured so much together just naturally do for each other.

Finally, the team begins to pray together beneath the stadium's glowing lights. For Will, it's an extension of a prayer he makes daily.

"I thank God every day that I have the chance to go out on that field," Will says. "It's an amazing feeling. It's just a great feeling to be on the field, to be a part of the team."

A prayer has been answered. A dream has come true.

✠

Invitation/Challenge: One of the mysteries and blessings of friendship is that people sometimes see in us qualities, strengths and potentials that we don't believe we have. Even when we resist, they keep seeing the best in us, and keep striving to help us discover our potential. I believe that's the way God approaches a friendship with us, too.

That approach to friendship also marks my book *When God Cheers*. A father is in danger of losing his close relationship with his child because he only sees success in sports through winning. A stranger enters the father's life, offering friendship and a different view of success—as a parent and as a person. A pivotal point in their relationship comes when the father says to the stranger, "You have more fun and more perspective at a game than anyone I've ever known. How did you get that way?"

The stranger responds, "Have you ever thought about when God would cheer?" After the father says, "No," the stranger continues: "Do you think he would cheer just for the team or the athlete that won? Do you think he would applaud just the game-winning home run or the 30-foot putt that dropped on the 18th hole? Would he only be thrilled seeing a swimmer earn another Olympic medal, a track star break a world record, a tennis pro win Wimbledon, or a volleyball team win a national championship? If you think about it, that approach is far too limiting for him, especially considering what he calls us to do in life. Sacrifice. Give completely. Commit yourself to others. Make the most of your talents. Reach out to your enemy. Be part of something bigger than yourself. Put everything you have on the line.

"The list goes on and on. And nothing on that list is easy. They're hard and demanding. And all those qualities can be part of sports. In fact, they are *the best part* of sports. *And* the best part of us. So God wouldn't cheer merely because some team wins or someone is a gifted athlete. He would save his best cheers for something more special than those measures of success. He would cheer for any team or any athlete of any skill level when they do in sports what he asks them to do in life. And he would cheer loudly. That's why I cheer the way I do."

Strive to reach your potential. Seek the best in yourself. Make God cheer.

PRAY LIKE YOUR LIFE
DEPENDS ON IT

Memories of her came back to him on the day he was to be married. He remembered her great beauty and her deep love for him, but mostly he remembered her incredible faith—like the night he was in the hospital, close to death.

"I was three years old with double pneumonia, and the doctor told my mother that I wasn't going to make it through the night," recalled Mark Williams. "She said, 'Is that your opinion?' He said, 'Yes.' She told him she was going to call another doctor for a second opinion—Dr. Jesus. She got in the bed with me. She prayed and prayed, all night long. The next morning, I woke her up. The double pneumonia was gone. She took me home that morning."

Leaving his home the morning of his wedding, Williams suddenly decided to take a photo of his mother to the church, never expecting that what happened there would touch so many people.

"I was born the last of 12 children," Williams said. "I was raised by a single mother. When I was born, I had sickle cell anemia. Because of her love for me and her desire for me to have a normal life, we grew so close. You would think that with 12 kids, it would have been catch-as-catch-can for her. But she permeated all our lives. Even with two heart attacks and diabetes, she maintained the household and the discipline. We all towered over her, but she ruled.

"She always said, 'Love is our foundation, wisdom our capital, truth our redeemer, pride our manner, Christ and education our salvation.' I used to say she had God's phone number. She'd pray and things would happen. There's one story that seems straight from the Bible, but it's true. For years, my mother had worked at the Army Finance Center, but then her body just broke down, and she went on disability. We were very poor, and one time there was nothing to eat. My mother picked me up in her arms, and we went to the front porch where she knelt down and prayed, 'Please, Lord, make a way for me to feed my children.'

"No sooner did she get up than a fish truck turned over in front of the house, literally spilling frozen fish on the street, sliding right up to the door. My brothers and sisters jumped off the porch, scooping up the fish. We ate well for weeks."

On the day of his wedding, six years had passed since his mother, Catherine Ludy, had died at 71. But Williams brought the picture of her to the Catholic church where he was ready to marry Jennifer Gray. As his mother's photo rested by his kneeler, Williams and Gray exchanged vows. After kissing his bride, Williams knelt and kissed the picture of his mother—a touch that left Williams' 11 siblings and nearly everyone else in the church in tears.

"I didn't plan to do it, but it just seemed like the natural thing to do," he said. "I had always planned for her to be part of that day, and there was regret and sorrow that she wasn't there. But I also felt she was there in spirit.

"I just wish I had acquired her faith. She just knew things would work out because she had God on her side. She always said, 'God and me raised 12 kids.' "

Invitation/Challenge: The journey of this book began with two images of two friends standing on the edge—of a cliff and a dance floor. In both situations, one friend invites and challenges the other to do something bold, to discover and embrace the breathtaking possibilities of life and love, while all the time asserting, "You can do this. Trust me. I'm here for you."

The journey of this book ends with two friends—God and a person—standing at the edges of life together, with one friend trusting the other so much that she places the complete well-being of her life and the people she loves into the hands of her friend, God. She knows that he has always been there for her. She believes that he only wants the best for her. So she willingly steps from the edge and takes the leap—into a forever friendship with God.

My prayer for you—and for myself—is that we do the same.

Acknowledgments

As a writer and a storyteller, I've been blessed to share the stories of many people who live their lives with a goodness and a dignity that are inspiring. *Then Something Wondrous Happened* features a small percentage of these people. Most of the stories in this collection were featured first in *The Criterion*, the newspaper of the Archdiocese of Indianapolis. A few of the stories initially appeared in *The Indianapolis Star*. To all of you who have given me the opportunity to tell your story through the years, thank you again. I have always considered your willingness to share and trust your story with me as an act of friendship. I have the same feeling for people who take the time to read the stories I share.

Thank you also to the many people who have blessed me with the gift of your friendship. At every stage of my life—including every school and every workplace—I've always been fortunate to share the journey with many fun, gifted and caring people, friends whose sense of humor is only surpassed by their sense of humanity.

A special thank you to my closest friends. Some of you I have been blessed to know for most of my life. Others of you have made me feel that I've known you for that long. One of you promised to share a life, and you have kept that promise.

To all of you, your grace helps me to remember my grace, and the blessing of sharing it. Your generous sharing of the journey has also made me feel even deeper the presence and the grace of God. Thank you for your influence. Thank you for your friendship.

Most of all, thank you, God, for the gift of friendship you offer all of us.

ABOUT THE AUTHOR

John Shaughnessy is also the author of *One More Gift to Give, The Irish Way of Life* and *When God Cheers.* A graduate of the University of Notre Dame, he grew up in the Philadelphia area and lives in Indianapolis. A longtime columnist and feature writer for *The Indianapolis Star*, he is currently the assistant editor and a writer for *The Criterion,* the newspaper of the Archdiocese of Indianapolis. He and his wife, Mary, have three children, John, Brian and Kathleen. They are also grandparents.

Made in the USA
Middletown, DE
20 May 2019